D O

Kenneth Stevenson is the Bishop of Portsmouth and a member of the Doctrine Commission of the Church of England.

A leading Anglican scholar, his many published works include *The Mystery of Baptism*, *The Mystery of the Eucharist in the Anglican Tradition* (co-authored with Henry R. McAdoo), *All the Company of Heaven* and *Abba Father*, all published by the Canterbury Press; and he was one of the compilers of *Love's Redeeming Work*, an anthology of Anglican spiritual writing published by Oxford University Press.

Reviews of other books by Kenneth Stevenson
available from the Canterbury Press:

Abba Father: Understanding and Using the Lord's Prayer
'Helps readers to realize just how precious a jewel the world
possesses in the Lord's Prayer.'   *CR Quarterly*

'For study or devotion this book can be thoroughly recom-
mended.'   *The Reader*

'All the way through, the stress is on letting the words of Jesus
speak to heart and mind.'   *Church Times*

*All the Company of Heaven: A Companion to the Principal
Feasts of the Christian Year*
'Has sparkle . . . maintains a lively interest throughout.'
                                            The Expository Times

'Could enliven a whole year's preaching and also provide
learning, refreshment and inspiration.'   *Theology*

'Communicates a real love for the liturgy as a means of
encountering the living Christ.'   *CR Quarterly*

The Mystery of Baptism in the Anglican Tradition
'Readers will be grateful for the skill and sensitivity which
links past concerns with present ones.'   *Ministry*

'We are led down many rich avenues of thought.'
                                        Church of Ireland Gazette

'Scholarly . . . well documented . . . helpful.'   *Theology*

'Contains rich and profound insights.'   *Search*

'A valuable resource.'   *Reviews in Religion and Theology*

To order these books, call our customer services on 01603
612914 or visit our website, www.scm-canterburypress.
co.uk

DO THIS
The Shape, Style and Meaning of the Eucharist

Kenneth Stevenson

CANTERBURY
PRESS
Norwich

First published in 2002 by the Canterbury Press Norwich
(a publishing imprint of Hymns Ancient & Modern Limited,
a registered charity)
St Mary's Works, St Mary's Plain,
Norwich, Norfolk, NR3 3BH

www.scm-canterburypress.co.uk

British Library Cataloguing in Publication data

A catalogue record for this book is available
from the British Library

ISBN 1-85311-464-2

Typeset in Britain by Regent Typesetting
and printed by
Creative Print and Design, Wales

CONTENTS

Contents

PREFACE

The advent of *Common Worship* (CW) marks a significant step for the Church of England, not least in eucharistic worship. How we celebrate the Eucharist matters a great deal, and how we think about what we are doing when we 'do this' is not a question to be left to other people. The Eucharist is what the People of God gather to do because it is the way in which we renew our covenant with the Lord, the same covenant made by us at our baptism. To walk past the font is to be recalled to that once and for all sacramental washing. To walk up to the altar-table past the lectern and the pulpit is to be put in the position of being fed with the food and drink of unending life in Christ.

But the ways in which this is done have varied – and rightly so. There is an inbuilt sense of the provisional about forms of worship for, unlike the Bible, they do not possess canonical status among us. We may cherish certain parts, and we have a right to expect the energy of Spirit-filled tradition to produce certain norms, whether in the basic shape of the service or of individual items like the eucharistic prayer. But different ages have different perspectives, and our own age is no exception.

As the title of this book suggests, the pages which follow attempt to locate the Eucharist in some kind of a context, using the *Common Worship* Order One as the base line. This is probably going to be the most extensively used form

in the Church of England; and it also has the advantage of
closely resembling the contemporary eucharistic rites of
our ecumenical partners, to say nothing of the Eastern
Churches, who have retained so many features of early
tradition that we have lost and have now recovered. We
shall also see this new liturgy in its historical context, as
part of the Anglican family of rites emanating from the
Christian West of today. And in so doing, we shall use
many writers, devotional as well as theological (the best are
both!), to illuminate what it is that we are trying to do at
the Lord's Table; there will thus be a good mixture of
names, ancient, medieval, Reformation and modern, who
will be called upon at regular intervals to cast a (sometimes
slantwise) light on the aspect or part of the liturgy under
discussion.

In Part One, we shall look at *Features* of the Eucharist.
The first four are about *Use*, such as shape, contexts,
variables and points when something is going on, and
words are found to cover (or conceal) them. Although there
are theological issues raised here, they have of necessity a
practical and pastoral outworking, even when set against
what the traditions have to say by way of explanation or,
on occasion, complication. The second four are about
Doctrine, and concern such central questions as symbolism, memorial, presence and kingdom; the Eucharist is a
profoundly symbolic activity, both in its language and its
actions, and at its heart are questions about how we
celebrate the death of Christ, how Christ is present with us,
and how his kingdom is inaugurated at the eucharistic
banquet. Not every eucharist can – or should – try to say
everything. But our age seems to look at the residue of
centuries of tradition with its own way of selecting what is
most important for its needs; and perhaps these include a
greater stress on the corporate, an imaginative way of

relating to language and symbol, a conviction that the Holy Spirit is a driving force in the world, not just the Church, and an awareness of just how fragile our lives are. If there is one truth we need to learn, it is to value and cherish what we have, rather than try to dominate it by understanding or manipulate it by choice. All those variable items are there to help us, not to confuse or bore us.

In Part Two, we shall look at the *Ingredients* of the Eucharist. The first four – approach, word, creed, intercession – are about the Liturgy of the Word. But just as the whole liturgy begins with what is called 'The Gathering' and ends with 'The Dismissal', so these ingredients need to be looked at in a more elastic fashion than we have sometimes allowed ourselves in the past. Worship arises out of our lives – hence the importance of preparation. The Word of God is not an arid exercise of the intellect, but a supple activity of the imagination. The Creed needs to be owned as the possession of the whole Church, primarily baptismal in its origin, rather than as a series of concepts to which we ourselves must either subscribe by personal agreement or not as the case may be. And the intercession, the locus above all of our self-offering (rather than our word-offering), is where we can have the space to dwell on the meaning of the gospel for the whole world, in the communion of saints.

The second four ingredients – offertory, eucharistic prayer, communion and conclusion – take us to the banquet table, in the Liturgy of the Sacrament. First there are preparations to be made, starting with the greeting of unity and reconciliation, and only then of the table itself – an area where perhaps there needs to be less fuss than there often is. After that comes the eucharistic prayer, the uniquely eucharistic proclamation of what God has done and continues to do for us; among all the variables in the new liturgy, this is probably the place of most spiritual richness

and potential confusion, which is why we have included an
Excursus that provides a more focused discussion of each
of the eight prayers. The Communion itself is signalled by
the recitation of the Lord's own Prayer, in which we pray
for bread for today, forgiveness for yesterday, and protection in the future – at this table. And the liturgy concludes
with pause for reflection on what it all means and prayer
for blessings in the future – chief among them the next time
we come back for more.

No liturgy is ever going to be perfect. Indeed, the last
thing this book encourages is some kind of ceremonially
slick and personally detached celebration in the course of
which nothing ever goes wrong. What it does hope for is a
more thoughtful, reflective approach to the Table of the
Lord, an approach which is patient about hidden truths
and ready to go back to words and actions that were once
thought to be fully understood in order to let them speak in
new ways and with richer meanings.

In putting together these pages, I am conscious of the
many different contexts in which I attend the Eucharist,
whether as president or not. I want to thank the many
people of the Diocese of Portsmouth who faithfully gather,
week by week, to 'do this', in all manner of different communities – whether it is the informality of a church plant,
the quietness of a rural parish, or the spacious warmth of
the Cathedral. For the past six years, these have been the
welcome, prayerful and thoughtful contexts in which I
have found myself taking part. As always, special thanks
must go to my diocesan colleagues, Mervyn Banting,
Christopher Lowson, Peter Hancock and Michael Jordan,
as well as Andrew Tremlett, my Chaplain, who presides
day by day in my chapel here at Bishopsgrove; to my friend
and ecumenical partner, Crispian Hollis, the Roman
Catholic Bishop of Portsmouth; to David Stancliffe,

Chairman of the Liturgical Commission, as well as to
Christopher Cocksworth, Colin Buchanan, Paul Bradshaw,
Michael Perham and Bryan Spinks; to colleagues on the
Doctrine Commission, especially Martin Kitchen, David
Ford, Ann Loades, Al McFadyen, Anthony Thiselton,
Richard Bauckham, Peter Selby, Geoffrey Rowell and
Stephen Sykes, for their patience with a historical perspec-
tive that needed stretching; and above all to Sarah, who
allowed me to gestate in sometimes long periods of silence
the ideas which follow, and to whom this book is dedi-
cated.

Kenneth Stevenson
Bishopsgrove
Fareham
Epiphany, 2002

PART I

FEATURES, PASTORAL AND DOCTRINAL

1 SHAPE

The need for shape

When I was a boy, my parents used to work together in designing panels of embroidery. One of these came into my possession. It consists of a series of patterns of different colours blending in and out of each other. The patterns come in two main shapes, one of them rectangular, the other rounded, and since all of them vary in size and proportion, the result is an interesting array, a kind of argument, between the ordered, fixed character of the one and the sheer spontaneity of the other. Like any good piece of art, it suggests different levels of meaning, and the religious person can read into it a religious dimension.

I have gazed at it in every place I have lived, from my room in the university halls of residence, through our first home at theological college, to where we live now. The colours have faded over the years, as happens with embroidery, but the underlying theme remains, namely that order and spontaneity are part of the lives we lead. And this we can 'read' at many levels. Different personalities respond to particular situations in different ways. Some people respond by intuition, others by calculation, others again by judgement, and yet others by feeling. Whenever I meet a group of candidates before their confirmation, I nearly always ask them please to 'remember' the service for the rest of their lives. And if, as often happens, the conversation moves into how this should happen, all sorts of reactions come to the fore. Some of the older people keep a daily diary, others might jot down impressions of important events in a notebook, others again will want to savour particular aspects of the occasion on their own, and yet others will want to talk about it with others.

The interaction between these widely differing responses is nothing new. All it says is that people are different and that the repertoire of experiences which they bring – unconsciously as well as consciously – to a particular occasion are going to vary from one person or group to another. Nevertheless, when people come to worship there needs to be some kind of form to what goes on – a form which draws together both 'poles', the ordered approach and the spontaneous approach. In some Christian traditions, one is elevated well above the other, so that, for example, the act of worship is either so rigid and stiff that it lacks humanity, or it is so loose and free that it doesn't seem to get anywhere. Many of our so-called 'informal' services fall into both these categories, since they can be just as fixed as the most traditional liturgy, or they can just as easily drift through much song and lengthy prayer so that the end-result (at least for some) is lacking in depth.

The truth of the matter is that good liturgies, because they have to engage with frail and varied humanity, have to be able to appeal to a sense of order as well as a need for spontaneity. By 'order' I do not mean rigidity, and by 'spontaneity' I do not mean chaos. Good order allows for the things of the moment to surface, and good spontaneity respects form. The two cannot do without each other, and this will become even clearer when the place of variables comes into focus. Yet not every act of worship can be planned endlessly by a committee, for that would be a disastrous abrogation of the mission of the Church. There will always be those big occasions where a planning-group becomes essential, but for most of the time, the day-by-day, week-by-week eucharistic worship of the people of God has to rely on what is given. This is usually the result of a long process of evolution (previous experience over the years and centuries) as well as the particular needs and debates of the time (Synods and Commissions), not forgetting how that form and spontaneity are earthed in the particular locality (the parish's own evolving tradition).

Shortly after the Second World War, an Anglican Benedictine monk, Dom Gregory Dix, wrote a long (and, considering it was also a scholarly work, surprisingly readable) history of the Eucharist entitled, *The Shape of the Liturgy*.[1] In many respects, much of the work of liturgical revision that has taken place since that time in all the churches (not just Anglican) has not really recovered from it. Dix wanted to woo people away from the idea that the liturgy is exclusively about getting certain words right – whereas in fact it is about much more. Like so many things, the pendulum has gone too far in the direction of 'shape' rather than 'content'. Dix alerted people to the deep structures of the Eucharist down the ages, with a particular emphasis on antiquity, his first love. What is done is almost seen to be more important than what is said – which is a strong message for Anglicans, who have relied on a literary piety for a long time. Many have questioned what Dix said, but few would question that 'Shape' (which is something more amorphous than 'structure') is a necessity for a good liturgy. Shape provides form and order and also gives space for variability and spontaneity. Shape gives stability, so that when the people of God gather to break bread, they know roughly what is going to happen, even though they will come to expect adaptation to the environment and to the occasion. Nor will any shape do – there needs to be a of coherence, a sense that on most occasions things n in some kind of order.

Basic shape

How, then, does this 'shape' come into land at an informal celebration at home, a Sunday morning Eucharist, or a weekday side-altar mass? For if the shape is to have any reality, then it has to embrace all of those very different environments. From the earliest times, it has been clear that the Eucharist comes in two main parts, and although they have been variously named, one centres on the lectern or ambo and is concerned with the reading and preaching of the Word, whereas the other is centred on the altar or table and is concerned with the eucharistic meal. CW gives these two parts prominence by naming them (somewhat stylishly) the Liturgy of the Word and the Liturgy of the Sacrament. It is important to see them in that order, for one would not think of starting with the Sacrament and moving on to the Word. It is just as important to realize that they are equal partners – the Word is not a mere prelude to be gone through in order to get to something more interesting, nor is the Sacrament an adjunct to the really significant business of preaching. Thus, for example, both parts are presided over by the same minister, an ordained priest or bishop, who may delegate certain specific ingredients to others but not the presidency of either part, for to do so would convey the impression that one is subordinate to the other, which is not the case.[2] Ordained Presidency is vital, for it symbolizes the unity of each eucharist with others that are taking place, have taken place and will take place – in the communion of saints. Moreover, the cumulative effect of the 'iteration', the solemn repetition, of this shape cannot be underestimated, inculcating in people a deep, collective memory of a movement through the Scriptures and the central narrative of salvation in bread and cup. From childhood, I can recall different kinds of eucharistic celebration, from the occasional visit to the village kirk, through a cathedral mass in Chartres, to a Danish suburban Sunday morning. Whereas the details would differ (and be attractive – why should we all be the same?), the basic shape or form would always be there in the background.

Shape is also about adaptation, and one of the questions that faces an increasing number of congregations is how far to adapt the CW provisions for those occasions when the Eucharist is celebrated with congregations made up of a high proportion of people who are not used to any kind of sacramental worship on a regular basis. Shape offers an understanding of the irreducible minimum required; a high level of verbal and sung participation of a complex kind – including intercessions that are strongly locally focused – can sometimes exclude people. On the other hand, the temptation is to pare down the liturgy on all these occasions, deciding in advance what the congregation will understand, and this can come across as a patronizing attitude. People need to be stretched, and worship can become too cosy and 'affirming'. This raises other questions as well. As Jeremy Begbie remarks, 'eucharistic repetition both stabilizes and destabilizes, even though it can also "go flat", and that means, in musical terms, the need for a certain kind of improvisation'.[3] This does not mean the disposable text or the ephemeral prayer, but the capacity for responsible use of the tradition in a particular moment in time. That is the risk we take in having a set liturgy with so many options.

The Liturgy of the Word in CW is preceded by another principal part which it calls 'The Gathering', just as its Liturgy of the Sacrament is concluded by another which it calls 'The Dismissal'. These require some explanation. I suspect that they are there because the new liturgies are often regarded as functioning well in themselves but they begin and end badly. That is to say, we need to work harder at how we start, for sometimes we are not ready, and we also need to work harder at how we conclude because the Dismissal is not an announcement, still less an anticipation, of the coffee-hour, but a command to the congregation to go out in mission to the world. Gathering at the start and going out in mission at the end are thus highlighted – uniquely for our own time – as aspects of worship in which there are unresolved issues in our own discipleship. In times past they were not so emphasized, perhaps because people took them for granted, or else because they were better at them. Whatever the truth of the matter, they are on our own spiritual agendas and rightly so. As we shall see, whereas CW gives some assistance in how we gather, it cannot be prescriptive in how we are to interpret the Dismissal, for that is the local congregation's task, not the liturgy's. Thus these two added ingredients function rather like book-ends, the one indicating inauguration and the other indicating conclusion – of a work that goes on and on.

But in case the sense of shape is allowed to become too cosy and neat (there are churches where everything is so well-planned that a bit of me longs for something to go wrong!), two important cautions need to be registered. This overall shape of the Eucharist emerged from earliest times and with variations here and there is likely to remain much as it is – at least in basics – for the foreseeable future. But its function is to engage, not to become so bloodless and lifeless that it lives its own life in a kind of distant earthly sanctuary – whether of endless ceremonial or endless preachy words – and so disengages with the people of

God. The shape of the Eucharist is not about domesticating
the gospel in such a way that it becomes a pet of our own
cosseting. The shape is there to challenge and arrest – and
at times even disturb. People have been converted by hearing a particular gospel passage read – like Antony of Egypt,
who as a rich young man left church one day and took
literally Jesus' command to sell all that we have and give it
to the poor (Matt. 19.21). Secondly, the actions that we
perform and the words that we say are not random. They
have been carefully agreed and they are being constantly
reinterpreted in every generation precisely because the
liturgy is about God, his engagement with the human race,
his readiness to redeem and nurture us. This means that the
liturgy expresses doctrine. As Regin Prenter, a prominent
Lutheran ecumenist of the twentieth century, once wrote.
'the liturgy is the bodily form of dogma, and dogma is the
soul of the liturgy'.[4] God's particular engagement with us,
week by week, day by day, usually requires a shape, a form,
a pattern, into which particularity, locality and spontaneity
have their essential place.

Four-action shape?

'In that form and in that order these four actions consti-
tuted the absolutely invariable nucleus of every eucharistic
rite known to us throughout antiquity from the Euphrates
to Gaul.'[5] This is how Gregory Dix describes the 'four-
action shape' of the Eucharist, in which we *take* the bread
and cup, we *give thanks* over them, we *break* the bread, and
then *share* the consecrated gifts. Dix was writing at a time
when scholars were more confident about how the
Eucharist was celebrated in the first three centuries than
they would be now. Paul Bradshaw, among others, has
provided a healthy scepticism as we look at just what little

evidence we do possess for early Christian practice, whether it is in the description given by Justin Martyr in the middle of the second century or the sample eucharistic prayer which Hippolytus provides at an episcopal consecration liturgy.[6] Many would now regard these central words of Dix as overambitious, but they are in essence on target. In any case we needed to hear them because the head of steam was building up which produced so many new liturgies. The fruits of that movement speak for themselves; I remember working for a time at a Roman Catholic University in the Mid-West of the USA and being struck by the way in which Roman Catholics, Lutherans, Presbyterians, Methodists and Episcopalians were able to share the fruits of liturgical scholarship and interpretation in the ordinary eucharistic diet of worshippers in their churches every week. In the language of the debate about post-modernism, the shape of the Eucharist is the overarching 'meta-narrative' of Christian worship.[7]

The four-action shape may have been overstated, but the results for the whole of the eucharistic rite are beyond question. The Word and the Sacrament are presented with a starkness and a clarity which we did not have before. True, they were always there, but now they are given a greater verbal and symbolic pre-eminence and we are the better for it; whereas *The Alternative Service Book 1980* allowed more flexibility of shape in its forms of service, CW is firmer about what goes where and is therefore more likely to provide congregations with liturgical stability. Word emerges from Gathering, which now consists of the entire preparation in which forgiveness plays an essential part as the people of God are called to penitence, make their confession and are absolved of their sins. In that first main section, praise and adoration intermingle, colouring penitence with the love of God, and everything begins with the

Greeting, a statement that we are met in the name of God himself. Then the Word unfolds in a sequence that starts with the Old Testament and moves chronologically to the New, but gives the writings of the apostles to the churches a subordinate position to the Gospel reading. That prominence is given visual expression by the use of a special Book of the Gospels and the posture of standing up in order to hear the Gospel read – the words of Christ himself as narrated in the Scriptures. I have often thought of the Gospel and sermon in the first part of the Eucharist as corresponding to the eucharistic prayer and the distribution of communion in the second – the reading of the Gospel and the eucharistic prayer are both narratives that are proclaimed, whereas the sermon and the distribution are both about sharing that good news, that nourishment. And just as the first thing we are aware of when we come into the presence of God is our unworthiness (hence the confession near the start), so when the gospel is read and preached, we become aware of ways in which our life of discipleship can be applied, beginning with intercession, offering the needs of the world to God in faithful trust. So the Liturgy of the Word has a shape, an internal logic.

The same is true of the Liturgy of the Sacrament, which begins with the Peace, a sign of reconciliation and unity, and proceeds with the preparation of the altar. Straight away, the eucharistic prayer sings out the mighty works of God, focusing on Christ himself, whose offering made once for all we graciously recall on earth. Then, as if to highlight the centrality of the gospel-prayer, rich with its eucharistic allusions of the holy name, the coming kingdom, the doing of the will, the daily feeding, the reality of forgiveness, and protection in the future, we pray the words Christ taught his disciples before partaking of this heavenly food and drink, now made ready for all as the bread is broken and

the wine outpoured. And just as Gathering merged into
Word, so Dismissal grows out of Sacrament, as the people
of God make themselves ready to go out, blessed with the
strength to live the gospel life. It is not easy and should
never be too slick because, by engagement with this ritual,
we are laying ourselves open to changing our way of life,
with a shape, a form of liturgy that is about the cross,
which is never a cosy or comfortable environment in which
to reorientate ourselves. As the American Lutheran scholar,
Gordon Lathrop, has recently written, 'participants in
Christian worship are invited to experience ritual that
criticizes ritual'.[8]

2 CONTEXTS

Buildings and basic content

Buildings play a far more significant part in the impact of the liturgy than many of us realize. Personal reminiscences of services are more likely to refer to the place where it all happened than the occasion, still less the rite in question. I can recall, for example, a Sunday Vespers in Milan Cathedral many years ago and what stays in the memory is the fact that it happened in that great building, rather than when, and what exactly it was.

Buildings affect the way the liturgy is done, and a good rule of thumb is to go with the flow and use the building as an ally rather than as an enemy. For example, in some rural dioceses there is a legacy of great medieval churches (which were never full of people, except perhaps occasionally), and small congregations have to learn to use them imaginatively rather than be dwarfed and overwhelmed with their size. Often simple solutions can revolutionize peoples' attitudes, like using one part of the building for the Gathering and the Liturgy of Word, and a completely different part for the Liturgy of the Sacrament and the Dismissal. Similarly, there are big occasions when a church can be almost unpleasantly overcrowded, so that the congregation long for the Peace in order to move around! However, our main problem nowadays is sameness, a determination not to exploit the potential of a building because we have to sit in serried preferably at the back. Sometimes a little stimulus ιs needed in order to encourage people to see themselves as a congregation which gathers for worship, rather than individuals who come along for personal religion.

Any set form of service has to carry a great deal when faced with such an overwhelming pluriformity. Some traditions respond by insisting on a basic uniformity, as if to keep us all in order. The Orthodox Church is one example, where virtually all buildings are (by comparison with the Christian West) of the same proportions and the Sunday main liturgy is the norm, always chanted, always with incense, always with the procession with the Book of the Gospels near the start and always with the procession of the gifts before the creed and the eucharistic prayer. There are no concessions except in scale, and the result is a sense of unity which is unknown in the West. Any adaptation that happens is in scale, seldom in content.

In the West, however, there has been a far greater degree of pluriformity, and much as some would want to regulate this phenomenon, it is unlikely to go away. The Eucharist takes place in many different environments, from an informal house celebration, through the Sunday morning occasions, to the quiet side-altar masses. Those are what might be called three prototypes, and they can be expanded into others, such as a hospital bedside or the grand-scale outdoor extravaganzas. Clearly a congregation which lived with all these at one and the same time, or on alternate Sundays, would have to cope with overstimulation, if not spiritual indigestion. But the question that needs to be asked constantly is this: What is the selection of material from the existing rite that is most appropriate for the particular context?[1] It never ceases to amaze me how some congregations put up with the same kind of rite, regardless of the environment or the occasion, to the extent that you sense that the words are 'gone through' in order to arrive somehow at the finishing-post. A reminder, as a wise priest remarked in relation to morning and evening prayer, that 'It is more important to say the daily offices than to have said them.'

Those responsible for planning parish policy over worship need to look carefully at a crucial page in CW which provides what might be called an irreducible minimum.[2] This is not to suggest something different every time, but rather to indicate what the Eucharist is supposed to do and say, regardless of the occasion and the options permitted. The list is instructive.

> The people and the priest:
> greet each other in the Lord's name
> confess their sins and are assured of God's forgiveness
> keep silence and pray a Collect
> proclaim and respond to the word of God
> pray for the Church and the world
> exchange the Peace
> prepare the table
> pray the Eucharistic Prayer
> break the bread
> receive communion
> depart with God's blessing

People need to know where they are. This is part of the identity of any Christian community. Some traditions may give more weight to certain ingredients than to others; for example, there is a fashion for playing down public confession, and not all congregations will want to share the Peace in a physical manner on every single occasion. But Anglican identity, in addition to providing this basic ground-plan, also provides set texts, some of them with many alternatives, and the way in which this ground-plan takes life results from the combination of people, text and environment.[3]

Three examples from the past

How do we match the three prototypes (the house communion, the Sunday celebration, the weekday mass) with this irreducible minimum? This is more than a question of mechanics. It is about atmosphere and precedent. Fortunately, history provides good practice in this regard, and while the examples about to be quoted do not fit exactly into the contemporary scene, they can assist us in the way of discernment.

Second-century Rome

The first example comes from Justin Martyr, who was writing a defence of the Christian faith to outsiders in Rome in the middle of the second century. This is what he has to say about the Eucharist:

> And on the day called Sunday an assembly is held in one place of all who live in town or country, and the records of the apostles or the writings of the prophets are read as time allows. Then, when the reader has finished, the president in a discourse admonishes and exhorts us to imitate these good things. Then we all stand up together and send up [offer] prayers; and . . . when we have finished praying, bread and wine and water are brought up, and the president likewise sends up [offers] prayers and thanksgivings to the best of his ability, and the people assent, saying the Amen; and the elements over which thanks have been given are distributed, and everyone partakes and they are sent through the deacons to

those who are not present. And the wealthy who so
desire give what they wish, as each chooses; and what is
collected is deposited with the president.[4]

Justin is writing for the outsider, hence the plain language
which (one assumes) avoids technical language. We can
recognize the Eucharist immediately for what it is. Quite
what degree of formality is envisaged is not clear. Some
have idealized the apparently 'informal' worship of the
early Christians, but others have been more circumspect:
people who face persecution are more likely to have a set
procedure. Nonetheless, the picture which Justin paints
resonates not only with the 'irreducible minimum' of the
structure in the CW Eucharist, but also for those who plan
celebrations in less formal environments. There may not be
a lengthy sermon, the president may not recite a eucharistic
prayer 'to the best of his ability' (CW does not envisage
improvising this prayer, even according to the conventions
which were being worked out in those early times), and the
communion may not be taken by deacons to those unable
to be present. But the rest speaks volumes; there is no
entrance procession, the readings have an 'ad lib' character
to them, there is very little movement, and the whole event
does not appear to be carried out in order to be particularly
impressive – beyond the basics of gathering, listening, praying, greeting, preparing the table, giving thanks and sharing
the gifts. On the other hand, there is little that is introverted
about this celebration; there is an outward focus, a mis-
sionary element, a sense of being part of something much
greater. The house communion of today could learn from
this early prototype.

nd example reflects a different age and environ-
gether – the papal rite in Rome at the end of the
seventh century. *Ordo Romanus Primus* (The First Roman
Order) is a description of the papal liturgy and because it
takes place in a large building (one of the 'basilicas' of
Rome) and involves a large number of ministers (bishops,
presbyters, deacons, subdeacons, readers, acolytes and
singers) it is inevitably complex. What follows is part of the
offertory rite:

> The pope, after saying Let us pray, goes down at once to
> the senatorial area, the chancellor holding his right hand
> and the chief counsellor his left, and receives the offerings
> of the princes in the order of their authorities. After him
> the archdeacon receives the flasks and pours them into a
> larger chalice held by a district subdeacon. He is fol-
> lowed by an acolyte with a bowl outside his cope into
> which the chalice is poured when it is full. The district
> subdeacon receives the offerings from the pope and
> hands them to the subdeacon in attendance, and he puts
> them in a linen cloth held by two acolytes. After the
> pope, the bishop on duty that week receives the rest of
> the offerings, so that he may put them with his own hand
> into the linen cloth which follows him. After him the
> deacon who follows the archdeacon receives the flasks
> and pours them into the bowl with his own hand.[5]

We have moved far from Justin's apparent simplicity! But
we must note that whereas Justin was writing for outsiders,
the author of this document was performing a different
task, namely to ensure that everyone knew what they were
doing in a complex series of relationships in an impressive
building. And the words 'relationships' and 'building' are

crucial, for the pope is surrounded by different mini/ who either attend upon him or who stand in some other kind of relationship to him in the ordering of church life in Rome, to say nothing of the nobility, who have a promi- nent place in the provision of the eucharistic gifts. It is as if the whole of Roman civil and ecclesiastical society has a role to perform. Moreover, the environment is more styl- ized; the irreducible minimum of Justin's account is dis- cernible between the lines of this rich ceremonial, but we have moved into a different liturgical world altogether. There is plenty of space, with an apse behind the altar from which the pope presides for the first part of the Eucharist, and there is a podium in the nave from where the singers chant and the readings, now set for each occasion, are read. Processions undergird the service, whether of the entry of the ministers at the start, the gifts at the offertory, or the communicants themselves later on.

Different as this milieu is, it still has a great deal to teach us, namely that if we are going to celebrate the liturgy in a generous liturgical space, with an array of different ministers (president, deacon, reader, churchwardens, choir), then it is essential not only that people know what they are doing (it is a fundamental law of liturgy that, like formal speaking, it usually takes a lot of work to make it look simple), but that what they do reflects their inter- relatedness. I recall once describing to a new curate what the main Sunday Eucharist was about in a parish I once served – not a whole lot of ceremonial (it was much simpler than this papal rite), but a network of relationships. The basic rules of thumb are that the president needs to be exactly what the term implies, neither a dictator who does everything nor an aimless manager at the mercy of all kinds of extra ministers who seem to be trying to take over. When I was a boy, the Eucharist was usually a monologue by the priest; nowadays the pendulum has gone so much the other way that the Eucharist can be a cacophony of different ministerial voices, and I often wonder what those in the pew actually make of it all.

Fifteenth-century England

The third context moves away from the grand basilican celebration to the side-altar mass, from late seventh-century Rome to England in the middle of the fifteenth century; and from a detailed description of the offertory for clerical professionals to the personal devotions of the individual worshipper. The mass is said quietly by the priest at the altar, assisted by an acolyte, and far from participating actively, the worshipper participates passively, watching for priest and acolyte to move here and there, to make this or that gesture, in order to know thereby which point the mass has reached. As the priest stands at the foot of the altar steps saying his confession, the worshipper is taken through the penitential preparation as through the rest of the service – in devotional verse.

> I know to God full of might,
> And to his mother, made bright,
> And to all his hallows dear,
> In many sins of diverse manner,
> And to thee, Father ghostly,
> That I have sinned largely.
> In thought, in speech, in delight,
> In word, in work, I am to wit
> And worthy I am to blame,
> For falsely I have take God's name.[6]

This text is a gem. It is part of a vernacular tradition of devotional prayer based on and inspired by the Latin texts

being muttered at the altar by the priest. The language is
not the disciplined rhetorical style of the older liturgical
texts, such as the collect and what we now call the extended
preface. This is affective piety, avowedly personal, in which
the worshipper is drawn into the Eucharist not by taking
part in the actions (at a side-altar mass there is barely room,
so the priest and acolyte do it all) but by words. It is a kind
of piety that survived the Reformation into the devotional
language of the Prayer Book (for example, in prayers such
as 'We do not presume to come to this thy table . . .') and
which undergirded the 8 a.m. celebrations of previous
generations. But it is still alive today as a need among many
people, especially those who lead busy lives and need the
liturgy to provide devotional nourishment.

Three prototypes

These three texts – Justin's description, the details of *Ordo
Romanus Primus*, and the *Lay-Folks Mass Book* – provide
some clear signals for the three prototypes which lie behind
the CW Eucharist, namely the house communion, the
Sunday celebration and the side-altar mass. The first
requires simplicity – but it can perhaps learn from the
outward-looking character of Justin's account. The second
requires working at relationships between ministers – but
perhaps cutting down on the fuss of those who are in the
sanctuary. The third requires a different kind of simplicity:
it mustn't try to look like a poor relation of the Sunday
celebration, but instead needs to provide its own kind of
space, trusting liturgical words rather less and perhaps even
allowing the intercessions to be offered in silence.

All periods of liturgical change have the demerits of their
merits. We talk a great deal about pluriformity – but we
need to do more about it, and perhaps these prototypes will

provide something of the answer. We have a multiplicity of texts – but we do not always know how to use them, and using them sometimes means having the courage to stick to a basic pattern, a rhythm, rather than wanting to use everything all at once. No liturgy can be exactly tailor-made for the architectural setting in which it takes place, but at a time of change perhaps we need to fidget less and trust the liturgy to do its job more than we do – and that includes many of those off-the-cuff explanations that get in the way of things. As Aidan Kavanagh once wryly observed, 'Reverence is a virtue, not a neurosis, and God can take care of himself.'[7]

These three prototypes cannot be norms for today. All they can do is indicate in a suggestive way the complexity of the tradition, to spur us on to adapt the liturgy to changing situations. But this is not consumer demand so much as faithful discipleship. However mass-produced the service sheet may be as a result of the press of the computer button, the words spoken and sung have a power and a suggestiveness far in excess of the simple act of reading them from the script in order to utter them aloud. That is why rhythms are so important.[8] For the words of the liturgy – like all ritual forms – have the capacity to restructure the way we see reality – which, at the Eucharist, starts with how we relate to each other (forgiveness), listen to the story (the word), share concerns (intercession) and eat and drink together (communion). Our 'reader-response' to the texts of the rite in the context in which we encounter them is the best proof of how multilayered the Eucharist actually is.

3 VARIABLES

What is variable

When I was newly confirmed, what struck me most about the Eucharist was the fact that it varied little from one occasion to another, which meant that I came to value those relatively few indications of the distinctiveness of one service over against another. As far as the text of the service was concerned, all that seemed to change were the collect and readings, the colour of the vestments, and the hymns, not forgetting the sermon. There was a sense of rhythm, which was only interrupted by solemn seasons like the procession on Palm Sunday and the evening Eucharist (a real novelty then) on Maundy Thursday; we were made aware, too, that it wasn't normal practice to celebrate the Eucharist on Good Friday.

It is easy to play up the contrast with what we have now. Things were not that stable then, because experiments had started, like involving others in offering the prayer for the Church or replacing it with a short litany, or the innovation of the offertory procession, with the congregation bringing up the bread and wine – something that happened for the first time after a sermon explaining it; I cannot recall anyone objecting, because it made immediate sense. As I took a greater interest in music, with the rich repertoire of

hymnody that could be used to great effect, the liturgical
year began to impinge more on me.

The CW Eucharist emerges from the past as its own
particular corrective. It is tougher on shape than the ASB,
and that means that there is an inherent stability. People
know when to expect what – or they should. They begin to
realize that a shape is crucial to what we are doing. It makes
sense to have the intercessions after the reading and preaching of the Word – far more so than placing them at the
beginning. It makes sense to greet one another with the
Peace (whether by word only, or by gesture) as a sign of
reconciliation before the table is prepared – far more so
than placing it before communion, where it can be something of a distraction. It makes sense to pray the Lord's
Prayer just before receiving the holy gifts: the words are so
familiar from other contexts that it is important to use
them as a way of approaching the holy table. Stability,
rhythm and shape are vital tools in effective liturgy. But
they have become even more crucial in our own time
precisely because there is now so much more variety in the
individual parts of the service than there used to be; and for
that reason, a caution needs to be registered against even
those small loopholes of variation that CW permits, like
placing the confession later and allowing the Peace to take
place elsewhere. We need that basic unchangeableness of
shape, in order to cope with the now basic changeability of
individual ingredients.

What are these variable parts? Over and above collect
and readings (now on a three-year cycle) and the sermon,
just about everything else:

• the service can be introduced after the opening greeting
• there are two forms of confession in the main text, and
  six others among the supplementary texts

- the confession can be introduced in different ways, with four additional forms provided, as well as seasonal provision
- there are two extra forms of absolution among the supplementary texts
- the Nicene Creed can be replaced by the Apostles' Creed or by one of seven affirmations of faith, to say nothing of the interrogatory form of the Apostles' Creed, or the responsive and metrical versions of the Nicene Creed.
- there are different forms for the intercession – five texts are provided
- the Peace can be introduced in different ways
- there are twelve 'table prayers' for use at the offertory
- there are eight eucharistic prayers, with proper prefaces for use with A, B, C and E, as well as extended prefaces for use with A, B and E
- there are five additional forms of words at the distribution of communion
- there is a complete set of seasonal and occasional post-communion prayers
- in addition to the two ordinary post-communion prayers, there are four additional forms
- there are seven additional forms of blessing, over and above the forms in the elaborate seasonal and occasional provisions.

In the face of such variety, perhaps the argument for uniformity of shape is self-explanatory.

Decisions about variables

But there are two questions that need to be asked. Who decides the choice in these variations, and how should a congregation make sense of the wide limits of these provisions?

The first question can be answered in a number of ways. There are Principal Feasts and Holy Days like Christmas and Easter, as well as Festivals like the Conversion of Paul, which cannot be ignored. There are also Lesser Festivals like Basil of Caesarea and Commemorations like Lancelot Andrewes which cannot take a Sunday over but which may form an important part of weekday worship. For most of these, the blocks of seasonal material will be sufficient to start with, and much of this kind of choice is probably best left to the president on the occasion in question. In any case, much of this material involves variations in what the president says, not what the congregation says. Extending this a little further, perhaps a distinction needs to be made between seasonal and occasional variety: seasonal variety is often made up of givens (collects, proper prefaces), whereas occasional variety is of a different order because it embraces particular needs in the community at the time. Sometimes considerable sensitivity is needed in such ingredients as the welcome, the introduction to the confession and the intercessions (a local tragedy can be overstated or understated). There are subtle ways of weaving local or national concerns into the liturgy that are appropriate to the occasion. But mistakes can be made, which is perhaps why the apparently off-the-cuff but actually carefully prepared works best at the greeting or the confession; and that part of the service where custody of the tongue is more than ever at a premium – the intercessions – can fall victim to a long list of information-ridden woes, leaving the congregation wilting and yearning for some space.

The second question is more complex, for it leads to an important area where CW needs to be handled and introduced with some care. There is a strong case for scrutinizing those elements in which the congregation's words or responses vary and those where they do not. For example, the eucharistic prayers can sometimes involve different responses, so that if a congregation has, for example, Prayers A, D and G on three consecutive Sundays, they might have a right to feel burdened with too much variety, especially if no explanation is given as to why these prayers were chosen. Similarly, if different forms of confession and affirmation of faith are used in the same way, then again there may be questions about the criteria for this kind of selection. It is not enough to say that it doesn't matter; people have strong attachments to sacred words spoken by others on their behalf, including at the distribution of communion.

One solution is to keep these matters under review through consultation, so that the priest talks them through with a worship group, which perhaps needs to include liturgical non-enthusiasts, as well as with the ministerial team. But a fundamental principle is that people have a right to know why what is used, and there are many occasions when good, simple liturgical teaching has taken place by sermons and short articles in the parish newsletter. It is better to start with a narrow range of options and build outwards from that base than to dive in at the deep end and find the congregation and ministers not fully aware of where they are. Variable elements, therefore, are those which the president or another minister says and those which the congregation says either as a response or as a full text. Both require careful selection, and both can have different kinds of impact on the congregation.

To return to the three prototypes – the house communion, the Sunday celebration, and the weekday mass – different selections are going to be appropriate for these contrasting contexts. For example, the house celebration by a bedside probably needs to be simple and memorable (perhaps even using Prayer Book material), whereas a home group may want more interactive material, such as a responsive confession, affirmation of faith and eucharistic prayer. The Sunday celebration often runs the risk of trying to carry too much within its liturgical limits and perhaps needs more care than it often receives; there are hidden gems, for example in the alternative words for the introduction of the Peace, which may link in with the sermon. We are, after all, dealing with art and there can be times when things come together in a remarkable way because extra work has been put in to make this happen. When I was a parish priest, all those taking prominent roles in the Sunday Eucharist used to gather in a chapel for quiet meditation, shortened morning prayer and a 'briefing' about the service half an hour beforehand; the briefing provided a vital opportunity for the preacher to tell the deacon the text of the sermon in the gospel, for example, or for a message to get to the intercessor that someone on the sick list had just died. The weekday Eucharist often provides the chance for a celebration with more space and fewer words and less attention paid to the service-sheet. All these variables, however, need to take account of the fact that the liturgy is something which is done, not said, and different occasions, seasons and contexts will require different uses of space, colour and tones of voice – what Frank Senn has recently highlighted, as 'performance theory',[1] which is a proper attention to how these texts are performed, uttered, paused for, prepared for, and that includes the congregation as well. Music is an essential part of this, for it forms one of the variable characteristics of the Eucharist, whether listened to as an organ voluntary or sung as a hymn in more active participation.

Eucharists with other rites and sacraments

But there is a fourth prototype for the celebration of the Eucharist – when another sacrament or rite is included. This is part of the inevitable process of eucharistic renewal that has been so much part of the scene over the past thirty years, and yet one more reason for adhering to a single shape. In Anglican tradition, the Eucharist has always been celebrated as part of ordination. There are hints of its lingering use after the Reformation in the 1549 Prayer Book at marriage and funerals, but these did not survive long. And baptism is only directed to be part of Evening Prayer, from which it soon detached itself, resulting in that lingering association with Sunday afternoon in an often quasi-private context. Now all that has changed, and we have the opportunity to celebrate all the major rites of the Church within the Eucharist: baptism, confirmation, marriage, ordination, healing, funerals, as well as many other services, including the licensing of various ministries.

It is not always appropriate to celebrate the Eucharist with all these rites. One of the motivations behind the CW Baptism Service was the need for it to be able to stand on its own, with sets of readings and seasonal prayers that include the blessing of the water. The same is true of the confirmation service, which also has seasonal prayers. When it comes to marriage and funerals, the congregations can vary so much that it is sometimes easy to identify when a eucharist is appropriate and when it is not. All these services, including some local diocesan forms for instituting and licensing new priests, are able to stand on their own, or they can be included in the Eucharist. Two words of caution are worth making. One is the complaint sometimes heard of 'eucharist with chips' – that there is a danger of becoming a church where the only service is the Eucharist.

Compared with bygone days, this is a good fault, if it is a fault at all, and there are going to be those who will be firm that the Eucharist is the only context in which these central events can be fully and properly celebrated. But there are also those who want to urge a certain restraint in this regard, and they have their place too.

The other question concerns how these rites are accommodated within the Eucharist. Invariably if something special happens at the Eucharist, unless it is a seasonal occasion like Candlemas or Palm Sunday, it takes place after the sermon and before the Peace. Some, like marriage, ordination, healing and funerals tend to stand on their own, as they have congregations which gather specifically for those occasions. Others, like baptism and confirmation, frequently take place within the Sunday Eucharist, and they contain optional ingredients such as testimony, the intercessions and the commissioning. In any case, the Peace is so closely linked to baptism and confirmation at the Eucharist that intercessions could be deferred into the eucharistic prayer, especially where G is used. Decisions sometimes need to be taken about how to encourage people to keep coming to these services, since there is a certain tendency to stay away! As these new and richer services are introduced, it may be a wise course of action to omit some of these variable ingredients, at least on occasions when there are many to be baptized and/or confirmed. Two other factors help. One is a good rehearsal, so that people know when to move and where to stand. Another is the way the service begins: a word of welcome followed by a time of quiet is often appropriate, especially if the congregation is made up of different groups and families not altogether familiar with their surroundings.

It is right that the Eucharist should be variable, for that is what its many contexts require. A concern, therefore, is that the rich amount of material at our disposal is usefully prepared and prayerfully offered. And if there is rather more than many of us are able to use and pray, then a certain restraint and attention to the options which are already there will help to meet that context. For at the end of the day, there is an objectivity about the command to 'do this', as God himself takes the initiative to engage with us wherever we are, regardless of our circumstances. Such aspirations as these lie behind a memorable paragraph from the concluding chapter of Dom Gregory Dix's great work:

Was ever another command so obeyed? For century after century, spreading slowly to every continent and country and among every race on earth, this action has been done, in every conceivable human circumstance, for every conceivable human need from infancy and before it to extreme old age and after it, from the pinnacles of earthly greatness to the refuge of fugitives in the caves and dens of the earth. Men have found no better thing than to do this for kings at their crowning and for criminals going to the scaffold; for armies in triumph or for a bride and bridegroom in a little country church; for the proclamation of a dogma or for a good crop of wheat; for the wisdom of the Parliament of a mighty nation or for a sick old woman afraid to die; for a schoolboy sitting an examination or for Columbus setting out to discover America; for the famine of whole provinces or for the soul of a dead lover; in thankfulness because my father did not die of pneumonia; for a village headman much tempted to return to fetish because the yams had failed; because the Turk was at the gates of Vienna; for the repentance of Margaret; for the settlement of a strike; for a son for a barren woman; for Captain so-and-so, wounded and prisoner of war; while the lions roared in the nearby amphitheatre; on the beach at Dunkirk; while the hiss of scythes in the thick June grass came faintly through the windows of the church; tremulously, by an old monk on the fiftieth anniversary of his vows; furtively, by an exiled bishop who had hewn timber all day in a prison camp near Murmansk; gorgeously, for the canonisation of S. Joan of Arc – one could fill many pages with the reasons why men have done this, and not tell a hundredth part of them.[2]

4 SOFT POINTS

What is a 'soft point'?

The scene is a Sunday Eucharist and the offertory hymn is in full swing. People are singing with gusto and the liturgy has gone well. But some cracks are beginning to show. The Peace took longer than usual and the organist went straight into the hymn. The sidespersons took longer to start taking the collection, and because one or two of them failed to turn up and the congregation is larger than usual, it becomes clear that the hymn is not going to be long enough. Add to which there is a new curate, a freshly ordained deacon, who has sole responsibility for preparing the altar; she has not been properly rehearsed, and when the bread and wine reach her there seems to be everything to do at once. The vessels are placed one by one on the altar and the linens meticulously arranged. By this time the organist is running out of ideas for improvisation. Eventually the president stands behind the altar, but the vessels aren't in the middle and the book is just far enough away to be difficult to read. And somewhere or other some kind of offertory prayer was said, though it wasn't entirely obvious where, what or why.

What I have just described could qualify for an item in 'Not the Nine O'Clock Eucharist', for there is a dimension of the burlesque about it. But things like that do happen – I have been there myself and have either been one of the

victims or one of the culprits of the drama. And it points up
how important it is both to recognize the sheer simplicity of
the side-altar celebration, where only a few of these things
take place, and the need for good rehearsal and simple
time-and-motion studies when the liturgy is more large-
scale. For example, sidespersons need briefing before a big
service. There are simple ways of moving communion
vessels to the altar without taking ages about it. And one of
the benefits of the CW rite is that a single table prayer can
be used immediately before the eucharistic prayer.

A soft point is a stage in the liturgy when something
is being done which varies according to the scale of the
service and it is therefore impossible to legislate exactly
how to proceed. It is a term invented by Robert Taft,[1] an
American liturgical scholar who teaches at the Oriental
Institute in Rome and has written extensively on the
Eastern rites; his considerable grasp of contemporary practice is informed by a wide knowledge of other liturgical
traditions, how they have developed in the past, and how
some of those developments have obscured the meaning of
the rite. And that is precisely his theme – a soft point can
grow like Topsy, and can obscure or even dislodge what
was originally intended to happen. To change the imagery,
is the ceremonial tail wagging the liturgical dog? Why
should the offertory procedure be so lengthy when it is in
fact a preparatory rite, not a central one? We shall have the
chance to look in more detail elsewhere at the offertory, its
origin and evolution. But for now, it is worth registering
that critical message.

How many soft points are there in the Eucharist? There are
a maximum of eight:

• the entry of the ministers
• the procession of the Gospel

- the collection
- the preparation of the altar
- the breaking of the bread
- the distribution of communion
- the Dismissal

The significance of each of these events is that they are all a mixture of the functional and the symbolic. The ministers usually need to make some kind of dramatic appearance in order to signal the start of the service; not all of them need to be robed and Anglicans are known to be self-indulgent about processions; but the entry of the president with other ministers is an important signal that the liturgy is about to start and all that went before by way of preparation is over. In many places the Gospel procession is a dramatic event, particularly if the Book of the Gospels has been carried in at the Introit and placed on the altar; not every building can take an elaborate series of movements here, but it is a way of stating that the words of Christ as recorded in the Gospels have a pre-eminence over and above other biblical readings. The collection needs to be taken and gathered, because it is part of the response of the congregation to the mission of the Church; our Reformation forebears made it an essential ingredient of the service and it is thus both functional and symbolic. The preparation of the table began life as a func- tional event, as the narrative of Justin Martyr shows, but by the Middle Ages individual prayers said by the priest with sacrificial overtones gave this part of the service a marked theology. Contemporary Anglican practice often represents a tug-of-war between those who want to reintegrate such a late medieval theology of presenting the gifts and those who want to emphasize only the offering of money, and since the two take place at the same stage in the liturgy, there is an unresolved tension.

The breaking of the bread before communion is a functional necessity when there is one loaf and many people, a very biblical echo which has a symbolic interpretation embedded in the New Testament (1 Cor. 10.17); but it often takes on a new life, especially when there are many vessels in use, the very reason for the introduction of the Agnus Dei in the Roman rite at the end of the seventh century.[2] The distribution of communion is self-evidently a varied part of the service and, like the preparation of the table, it needs to work on a good balance of distributors (and distribution points) in relation to those who are present; by its very nature it is both functional (the gifts need to be received) and symbolic (the gifts are nothing less than Holy Communion). Finally, the Dismissal sometimes develops its own special momentum; it can involve the giving of candles to the newly baptized (the candles need to be lit and blown out before the service, so that they will light quickly during it) and at ordinations the new deacons and priests are often given their New Testaments and Bibles at this point; here are 'dismissal rites' which need to happen before departure from the sanctuary, and they are both functional and symbolic.

What to do about them

We are thus faced with quite a number of these soft points and, in every case, groups of people are involved in doing things and there are prayers which can or could accompany them. The much-loved collect for purity only became part of the beginning of the Prayer Book Communion rite because it was among the prayers recited privately by the priest as part of the preparation for mass in the late Middle Ages and was obviously thought too good to lose. Sometimes the president blesses the deacon before the reading of the Gospel, a late medieval custom which expresses relationality, and when the bishop holds the crosier while the Gospel is being read, this is a gesture symbolizing the bishop's teaching office. The table prayers in CW are an amalgam of material that either does not specify what is being offered, or refers to the bread and wine, or to the money, and in many respects it would have been better to have kept them all ambiguous; in any case, the oldest prayers in the Roman rite at this point often referred to offering the Eucharist in general terms, rather than explicitly to the gifts of bread and wine.[3] What is said or sung at the breaking of the bread clearly needs to 'cover' the required actions, and CW provides formulae that are appropriate at a simple celebration as well as the traditional singing of the Agnus Dei. As far as the distribution is concerned, what is really lacking is devotional material for people to use while others are receiving communion; while this is, strictly speaking, not part of the liturgy, it is still an area where many people would benefit from some assistance, particularly as Anglican liturgy has from the very beginning been able to embrace both 'public' and 'private' piety (the corporate text of the Church and the individual prayers of the believer) within its wide boundaries. Finally, the dismissal rites provide the right words, including those occasions when candles or bibles are distributed; it is just a question of getting the actions right and not turning the liturgy into a nonsense, for example by having the formal Dismissal before the final hymn, and thus sending signals of clericalization by insisting on the congregation waiting while the procession moves out.

These soft points are not to be derided. Their very intricacy and variety require attention both to the detail of what is done (how to move easily and without fuss) and to the most appropriate words to use. Soft points have a theology.

That much needs to be recognized. It is a question of exactly what that theology is! We all know that other parts of the service, like the absolution, the eucharistic prayer, and the blessing, are of central significance, and some people would give them all a prominence that would outshine other ingredients. These 'hard points' are given – they need to be said, like the reading of the Gospel and the sermon. But there is little action in them that needs tailoring to the building in the way that the soft points require, especially as soft points necessarily include other people, their movement, their interrelatedness, their co-operation, their partnership in the gospel. Those suspicious of cere-monial need particularly to take them seriously, if only to work even harder at them in order to make them simple – people are more likely to be fussy and self-conscious if they are unrehearsed and ignorant of what they are supposed to do and why they are there.

The theology of entry is a statement that the liturgy is beginning – whether you are at a home communion, a Sunday celebration, or a weekday mass. It is a question of working out what is most appropriate to the setting and ensuring that the movement – or lack of it – expresses the character of the community. The theology of the procession of the Gospel is a statement that a unique Bible reading is about to be heard – and that can be a counter-cultural action in the age of the paperback. The theology of the offertory is a statement about the importance of sacrificial giving – a sensitive matter as the Church of England slowly catches up with other Christian bodies in the matter of giving. The theology of the preparation of the altar is a statement about the need to make ready the holy table with love and reverence, whether it is a simple wooden structure on which ordinary bread and wine are placed in silence, or we are dealing with an elaborate altar with a lavish use of incense. The theology of breaking the bread is a statement about the meal being prepared for distribution, and there is a great deal to be said, for example, for using one chalice and one flagon at the eucharistic prayer and bringing forward other chalices only at this point, perhaps thereby making it even softer! The theology of the distribution is a statement that the gifts are there to be given and shared, an essential part of the Reformation doctrinal repertoire. And the theology of dismissal is a statement that we are called not to stay but to go out – in order to return again and again and again and be fed with the food and drink of new and unending life.

Pointing forward

It is no coincidence that each of these soft points is an act of preparation that leads to something else. The introit ensures that the Gathering will happen. The Gospel procession ensures that the most important reading will be attended to – and standing up for the Gospel is a dramatic moment with a cumulative impact. The offertory ensures that the mission of the Church is secured. The preparation of the altar ensures that the Eucharist can be celebrated. The breaking of the bread (and the pouring of the wine) ensures that the distribution can take place. The distribution ensures that the people of God are fed – and it is not just 'me', it is other people, with whom I am in communion, whether I like it or not. And the Dismissal ensures that we are all sent forth.

The fact that each soft point is both variable according to circumstance and by its nature preparatory does not in any way diminish its importance. But it does mean that there is a tendency for the movement to become top heavy. As Robert Taft points out, 'One of the most common phenomena in liturgical development is the steadfast refusal to let a gesture speak for itself.'[4] Liturgical fidgets are not only people who want to change things all the time; they are also people who do not trust actions to be sufficiently eloquent in themselves. There will be occasions – like Good Friday – when the Entry is impressively done in total silence. There will also be occasions – like the Easter Vigil – when the Gospel procession needs even greater drama, because so much has happened already with the sharing of the light and the Old Testament readings. There will be occasions when the collection needs to be sent round a second time because the People of God are ungenerous. There will be occasions when the new priest, faced with a tiresomely lengthy preparation of the altar, needs to simplify so that people can see what is going on unencumbered by a multiplicity of people moving around and not doing a great deal. There will be occasions when bread needs to be visibly broken (I have always had doubts about the need to say anything at this point). There will be occasions when the gospel imperative requires that those sitting at the very back are given communion first. And there will be occasions when the Dismissal could rightly consist of the whole community breaking up and going forth from every door in the building.

Soft points need watching. They probably repay more attention than any other parts of the service. They are about context. They are also about variability. At their worst they become what Bernhard Lang has described as 'liturgy in love with itself',[5] unrelated either to its own meaning or its proper mission. They are about trusting movement to speak for itself, provided that what is done is bold and visible. They are there because the God whom we worship is a God of movement, from one part of the Christian drama to another.

5 SYMBOLISM

Disability

Disability is a growing interest for many people and the disabled are given far more attention than in past ages, to the extent that we are beginning to realize that – in a sense – we are all disabled in one way or another, whether it takes the (serious) form of not being able to see or whether it takes the (much less serious) form of just not being able to handle a cricket ball, regardless of what people tell you to do. I have had many conversations with people who work for the seriously disabled, outstanding among them a time I spent with someone who works as a Chaplain to the Deaf. It was a fascinating experience, because all the time I became more and more aware of the fact that the deaf are dependent on the 'sign language' they come to know or the kind of gestures which require no interpretation, like holding someone's hand with the exchange of a smile. One of the souvenirs of that encounter was a copy of the Lord's Prayer in sign-language, two gestures of which stand out clearly – kingdom and temptation. Kingdom is expressed first by placing the right hand over the top of the forehead, and then by drawing both hands together, palms upwards and extending the fingers outwards. The first gesture suggests a crown and the second gesture engagement and involvement. Temptation is expressed by tugging the right lapel of the shirt backwards and away, as if we were being falsely distracted.

Both these examples of sign language demonstrate its basic need, to communicate with those who cannot hear. But they also show how rich the signs are in themselves, how eloquent they are in their simplicity. 'Keep it simple' is a motto frequently given to those of us who are in the talking business. This does not mean 'be simplistic' – which is what it often becomes. By simplicity – a gospel virtue – is meant a way of getting straight to the heart of the matter. This is why, for example, being simple sometimes means challenging (or even upsetting) people by the directness of what is said. That is one of the reasons why I always watch for the expression on the face of whoever is signing a speech (at a meeting) or a prayer (at a service). What we are trying to communicate with each other is more than can be put into words, and that is why we are all disabled when it comes to even imagining the things of God, let alone trying to find a language in order to put them into words.

Not being able to hear or speak is not the only major form of disability. There are those who cannot move easily – which means that points of access to church buildings become critical, and word soon gets round about which particular churches are unwelcoming in that regard. There are those who find it difficult to concentrate for long, or who cannot communicate what they want to say, or who cannot read what is in front of them because the order keeps appearing differently to them as they try to work out what it is saying. The community of L'Arche has for decades been a focus for reflecting on what it means to be disabled, to be, in words once used by Jean Vanier, 'founded on a broken body'.[1] There are those for whom music is a closed book because they cannot tell the difference between one

Symbolism

note and another, to the bafflement of those of us for whom
music is a way of life.

There are also those for whom the Christian faith is itself
the main obstacle, because they have been disabled by
earlier experiences. Here the repertoire is endless. I was
forced to go to church when I was young and nothing will
make me go now. I heard stories about child abuse in that
church and I know that the victims and their families will
never get over it. A cousin committed suicide and I don't
know how a loving God can let that happen. I was in a bad
road accident and escaped – but my wife and family did
not. And the disabilities can become more focused: Why all
this rigmarole in church? I don't like happy-clappy worship
and those plastic smiles. Going up to communion and being
given a piece of bread and a sip of wine seems bizarre to me,
as a Jewish friend of mine once told me.

The language of symbolism

All these attitudes, conditions and reactions add up to the
same truth: in the business of trying to be Christian, we
have to try to enter a different world in order to explain our
own, in all its dimensions of limitation, creativity and dis-
appointment. As Dietrich Bonhoeffer discovered in the very
different circumstances of trying to be a Christian in Nazi
Germany, you cannot have God without the world, and
you cannot have the world without God.[2] It is a world of
symbolism, a word which means throwing things together
and holding them there. This is not the world of the start of
the television news bulletin, with a snap summary of the
main items that are somehow going to be dealt with at
greater length later on. And there is a distinction between
a sign and a symbol, because a sign says exactly what it
is, like 'no entry' at the end of a street, whereas a symbol

expresses more than what is obvious, like a warm hand-shake. As Timothy Fawcett pointed out some time ago, there are many differences.[3] For example, signs operate at the level of object-thinking whereas symbols push us beyond empirical objectivity towards an appreciation of the transcendent. Signs have only one meaning, whereas symbols can have many layers of meaning and resonance. Signs are invented by convention, whereas symbols simply emerge. Signs operate only in relation to what is signified, whereas symbols operate only insofar as they have a multiple relation to what is signified. And signs do not ask for commitment to what is signified, whereas symbols are born in and for an encounter.

Symbolism pervades our use of language too. To take the most obvious example, the death of Christ is more than a sign that someone has died, because it is a symbol of cost and victory. It also places the bread and wine of the Eucharist as more than a sign of the availability of food and drink, because they are symbols of new life now, a journey with many further explorations to be made. It also elevates those 'signs' used for the deaf and hard of hearing to the level of symbols, like the twofold gesture of hand on head and two hands turned outwards with fingers outstretched, because they indicate far more than an immediate message. In fact, they are just as eloquent about the truth they suggest as about the word – kingdom – which they are supposed to represent. As David N. Power has written, 'Symbols in the cultural sense have to do with the world as meaningful, whereas the kind of signs from which they are separated have to do with making living in the world functional.'[4]

But words still matter, because the Christian faith needs to be reflected upon in company with others – and communicated. There would be no point in abandoning their use altogether, otherwise what we say and how we say it would degenerate into a vague 'spirituality' that had no sharpness, no requirement of commitment, no commonly held coherence. So we remain part of our own world, the world of the apparent and the obvious, but also the world of symbolism and the less obvious, a world in which we are all disabled to a greater or lesser extent. And because we are all disabled, not fully able to comprehend God, nor fully able to make sense of our actual world, what we say about our lives, and our need for nourishment and sustenance, is going to be limited and imprecise. If we try to take the world of obvious signs into a way of looking at life which is fed by the less obvious means of symbolism, then we are presenting God with an insuperable obstacle – not our own disability, but a real and wilful inability.

Liturgy is its own language, the language of symbolism, in which the new creation is continually being celebrated, directed, and given meaning. And the Eucharist is the central way in which that celebration, direction and meaning are focused, because the bread and wine are the nourishment and sustenance of the Christian journey. Unlike other symbols, such as being given the keys to the car when I passed my driving test in order to express access to the vehicle in a role no longer always that of a passenger, the Eucharist meets many different aspects of life, for which an increasing degree of provision is made in the new forms of liturgy. The inherently variable aspect of the Eucharist is its own essential genius. At its heart lie two elements, bread and wine, which are spiritual food and drink. They convey their own eloquence by virtue of the fact that each eucharist is connected to another – the command to 'do this *as often as* you drink it' is a way of saying that it is part of life, ordinary but special, to be repeated regularly; not to be taken for granted, nor left to become so special that it is effectively unattainable. As Richard Hooker, the great Elizabethan divine, once wrote, 'Such as will live the life of God must eat the flesh, and drink the blood of the Son of man, because this is a part of that diet which if we want [lack] we cannot live.'[5]

Bread and wine are made for symbolic application. They are food and drink. But they are food and drink of a particular kind and with a particular consequence. Bread and wine are themselves the result of the process of crushing corn and grapes, mixing yeast with the former and allowing the latter to ferment;[6] there is a pattern of dying and rising in the production of these elements, which we have to make for ourselves – they are not fruits of the earth that come to hand with the seasons. And the bread is then broken and the wine poured out in order to be shared. Something of this is suggested by the two formulae in CW at the breaking of the bread: the first speaks of those who are to partake as being 'one body', and the second asserts that 'we proclaim the Lord's death until he comes'. This food does indeed nourish, but its very existence is the result of a process of baking and fermentation which is also about our co-operation and dying and rising. Many writers down the ages have drawn attention to what is sometimes called the connection between 'symbol' and 'similitude'. For example, Hugh of St Victor, a canon of the Victorine Abbey in Paris and one of the most remarkable theologians of the twelfth century, once wrote: 'The apostle clearly states that Christ's death and resurrection is a sign, a similitude, a representation, a sacrament, an example. Cannot the sacrament of the altar be a similitude and also a truth?'[7]

Symbolism and the eucharistic meal

The bread and wine need words, in order to surround the celebration with a coherence, a meaning. I was once present at a silent eucharist. It was at the end of a series of house group discussions and we were tired of talk. Not that the talk had been without value, but we realized that our words were insufficient. It was a one-off, and it could only be done with a group of people already tightly bound together by a common occasion, a common intent. The majority of us have to rely on words, even though we learn, especially with people we love, that words sometimes get in the way. So in the liturgy, words have to be used and they come at us sometimes thick and fast, sometimes quite sparingly. In recent years, there has been a deliberate attempt to enrich the language, so that it sounds less flat than in the earlier attempts at modern English over thirty years ago.

The ancient hymn, Gloria in excelsis, originally written for the Greek office of mattins in the fifth century, is – like the eucharistic prayers – a powerful focus of symbolic language. The opening lines contrast the height of God's glory with the gift of peace on earth, echoing the song of the angels at Christ's birth (Luke 2.14). 'The highest' is not a physical statement of God's measurability but rather a way of pointing to his difference. The second section refers to God in the traditional language of lordship and kingship, which inspires awe – a theme at the heart of this hymn – and to whom we owe worship, thanksgiving and praise. These three are not exactly the same; worship is an attitude of the whole person, thanksgiving is about what God does for us, whereas praise is what God is in himself. These are little words with big meanings. They are symbols of wider and deeper truths, not sign-posts to immediate action and application in a narrowly defined way.

Then the hymn moves on to address Christ, who is the way in which God reveals this distant glory in our midst, the centre of our worship and thanksgiving. Once again, the symbolic language comes at us – Lord, Christ, God, Lamb of God. All these words are about difference and identification, which is the very truth which Christianity proclaims: the high and mighty God showing us his human face in Jesus the Christ, who is therefore both Lord and Lamb of God. And the hymn goes on to sing the prayer for mercy and healing for our sins, and at the same time to recognize that this eternal Lamb has not only taken away our sins but is seated at the right hand of the Father (Rev. 5.6). The Lamb who was slain is alive, and the symbol of the 'right-hand' indicates strength and privilege, on equal terms with God, hence the attitude of being seated.

The final section is a further act of praise. Jesus is the holy one (Luke 4.34), the Lord, the most high, with the Holy Spirit, in the glory of the Father. The hymn emerged from a time when there were those who wanted to distance Jesus from God and were unsure of the place of the Holy Spirit. Thus it provides a hymn of praise to the Trinity, focusing on the work of Christ. It is no surprise, therefore, that it came West and embedded itself in the start of the Roman mass, first of all at episcopal eucharists at Christmas, then spreading to Sundays and feasts regardless of who was the president.

The Gloria in excelsis presents us with symbolic language and our response can vary from being overwhelmed or patient. In some charismatic congregations, this is the stage in the Eucharist when there is a time of 'worship' – extended praise, rich in symbolic language of its own kind. We are disabled to comprehend what it is trying to say, but that is no reason for being unable to enter into it at all. Symbolic language requires a readiness to engage at different levels

with what those symbols of height, peace, heaven and glory
are about. Moreover Jesus, who is described as Lord and
Christ, by virtue of being the Lamb who has taken away
our sins and who is now at God's right hand, could just as
easily be called a living reality and nothing more. But that
would impoverish how we speak of the things of God,
because there are many other living realities to our daily
existence, like the need to be careful when crossing a road
with busy traffic. We need this rich symbolic language,
perhaps not as an immediate point of access to Christian
faith, but certainly as a regular diet, to ponder rich meanings alongside that bread and that cup. [8]

6 REMEMBRANCE

Anamnesis

'Who, in the same night that he was betrayed took bread and gave you thanks . . .' These words lie at the heart of every eucharist. They are more than 'mere words', for they are an indication of what is to follow: the words and actions of Jesus with his disciples in the Upper Room. It is important to have these 'cue words', because in the rhythms and repetitions of communal actions we learn to know what is coming. They are in the centre of the eucharistic prayer and take the worshippers from their own words to Christ's words.

The words are not always the same. Indeed, if you compare the four versions which appear in the New Testament, you will find some significant differences. For example, whereas Mark and Matthew portray Jesus refusing to drink from the fruit of the vine until the time of the kingdom (Mark 14.25; Matt. 26.29), Luke and Paul give us the command to repeat – 'do this in remembrance of me' (Luke 22.19; 1 Cor. 11.25). Paul's narrative comes in the First Letter to the Corinthians during a discussion about right procedures and relationships at the celebration, and is widely held to be the earliest of the four. That doesn't necessarily make it the most important, but it is the one which lies behind the various versions which have appeared ever since in the many eucharistic prayers,

Aramaic, Greek, Latin, German, English, Inuit. The command to repeat makes sense. The experience of the Church in commemorating his death and celebrating this holy supper requires it.

The word 'remembrance', an old English word, is a difficult term. It is an attempt to translate the Greek word, *anamnesis*, a term from philosophy which is about drawing from the memory, usually something vivid and powerful, and relating it to the present day. Its use in the New Testament, however, takes us to the Jewish roots of Christianity, for in the Old Testament, the Hebrew word for memorial (e.g. of the Passover) is *zikkaron* – and to celebrate the Passover was far more than a mental act (Exod. 12.14, 13.9). It was – and is – like bringing a past event of universal significance before God in solemn thanksgiving in such a way that its consequences take place now. It is not difficult to see why the early Christians latched onto this dynamic understanding of remembrance, particularly as the event which the Eucharist proclaims can be seen as the Christian Passover. 'Our paschal lamb, Christ, has been sacrificed', as Paul points out a few chapters earlier in the same letter (1 Cor. 5.7).

We are back with the problem of how to put into words what words cannot express. And the dangers of misunderstanding what might be called 'the dynamic of remembrance' are considerable, particularly if there is a tendency to internalize religious experience and turn all prayer into mental activity. Christ then becomes so firmly nailed to the cross that he has no life among us. All we have to do is surrender ourselves to the cross – and as a result live lives that are spiritually rather passive. But there is an equal danger in turning this remembrance into something so dynamic, dramatic and powerful that it looks as if we are the actors, and the Eucharist is all about us. The sheer centrality of the cross of Christ can become lost in the mists of an impressive liturgical performance, and the cost of discipleship subsumed under the garb of an ecclesiastical show.

I exaggerate in order to make a point – which is that the remembrance of Christ is fundamentally *his* action in us now, and that is why it is so important to move from *our* words to *his* at the heart of the eucharistic prayer. Of course, the words of praise and thanksgiving, prayer and intercession which surround the narrative of the institution are central too. We need a context in which to place this narrative, otherwise it would appear rootless and vague. We are not back there in the Upper Room, re-enacting the meal as if it were a drama on the stage that we somehow had to try to enter, like actors watching each other with a degree of self-consciousness. The drama takes place *now* and in our time. It is historical, in the sense that it points back to the cross, which looks backwards to the Last Supper and forwards into the resurrection life. But it is also contemporary, in that the Eucharist is about our life being redeemed, the suffering and pain of our time being pointed to the future in mercy and judgement. The Anglican–Roman Catholic International Commission wrestled long and hard with the divisions of the past in relation to this question, and emerged with a simple but strong formulation, very much akin to the early Christian Fathers as well as the classical Anglican divines:

> The eucharistic memorial is no mere calling to mind of a past event or of its significance, but the Church's effectual proclamation of God's mighty acts. Christ instituted the eucharist as a memorial [anamnesis] of the totality of God's reconciling action in him. In the eucharistic prayer the Church continues to make a per-

petual memorial of Christ's death, and his members, united with God and one another, give thanks for all his mercies, entreat the benefits of his passion on behalf of the whole church, participate in these benefits and enter into the movement of his self-offering.[1]

The balanced and powerful language of this and other ecumenical agreements is echoed in most of the new eucharistic prayers and implicit in the shorter ones. To be drawn 'into the movement of (Christ's) self-offering' is to say that we are being offered to the Father – through him alone.

Although the whole eucharist is an 'anamnesis' of Christ, there is rightly a focus in the particular paragraph which follows the narrative of the institution in the eucharistic prayer. This is usually referred to as the 'anamnesis', because it 'remembers' the death and resurrection of Christ, which are central to what the Holy Communion is about. But of course 'anamnesis' is far wider and deeper, as the seventeenth-century priest and poet, Thomas Traherne wrote:

Had the Cross been twenty millions of ages further, it had still been equally near, nor is it possible to remove it, for it is with all distances in my understanding, and though it be removed many thousand-millions of ages more is as clearly seen and apprehended. This soul for which Thou diedst, I desire to know more perfectly, O my Saviour, that I may praise Thee for it, and believe it worthy, in its nature, to be an object of Thy love; though unworthy by reason of sin: and that I may use it in Thy service, and keep it pure to Thy glory.[2]

The Last Supper is shot-through with the atmosphere of sacrifice. This is not only because Christ's death is imminent and we therefore necessarily celebrate the Eucharist in the shadow of the cross. It is because we keep being drawn into faithful discipleship through Christ's self-offering. Of course, as Timothy Gorringe has recently pointed out, 'the gospel is not about the importance of being earnest'.[3] But faithful discipleship is costly, as Paul indicates when he coins that extraordinary expression, 'living sacrifice' (Rom. 12.1), which suggests that the Christian life is about dying and yet living, an offering of ourselves in joyful obedience. This takes us back to another sacrificial theme which is mentioned in the narrative of the institution – covenant: the new covenant in Christ's blood.

Covenant is a legal term, concerning agreement. God established a covenant with Noah (Gen. 6.18) and with Abram (Gen. 15.18) which then became the foundation of the relationship between the People of Israel and their God. If the people obeyed the statutes of the Lord, they would be cared for and looked after, but if they did not obey them, then God would forsake them – as was made clear to Moses on Mount Sinai (Exod. 19.5). But the covenant kept being broken and it was only in the tragedy of exile in Babylon that the prophet Ezekiel prophesied that there would be a new covenant, for the Lord would remove from his people their hearts of stone and instead give them hearts of flesh (Ezek. 36.25ff.) and make for them an everlasting covenant (Ezek. 37.26). It is this new covenant which Jesus makes, with his own blood. It is an agreement signed not in ink but in the cost of his own life. The new covenant in Christ's blood is mentioned in each of the four New Testament versions of the narrative of the institution (Mark 14.24; Matt. 26.28; Luke 22.20; 1 Cor. 11.25).

Covenant may be a legal term in origin but by now it has become a fundamentally religious one as well. It is about the shifting dynamics of the relationship between the people and their God. It is no longer about specific, binding contracts, because human beings are incapable of living up to them – that is, if those binding contracts are of any last- ing significance. So the dynamic shifts in order to allow for the reality of the demands of the Kingdom of God and the reality of our capacity for sin. We can enter into a covenant with God and we can renew it when we have broken it. That is not an easy way out. It is about accepting the full depth of the love of God, who longs to bring us back to him, as well as about accepting the full depth of our weak- ness and our desire to make sense of the confusions and contradictions of the lives we lead.

This dynamic, therefore, of entry and renewal is expres- sed in the two foundational sacraments – baptism and eucharist. As Herbert Thorndike, another seventeenth- century theologian, once wrote: 'The necessity of the sacrament of baptism and of the eucharist unto salvation consisteth in the covenant of grace, in which our Saviour consisteth; and which the one of them setteth and enacteth, the other reneweth and re-establisheth.'[4] The Eucharist as the renewal of the covenant is a constant theme in the works of Thorndike and many other writers of his time. Such an emphasis helps us to see the point of those words, 'the new covenant', as they appear in the eucharistic prayer. It also helps us to see the whole Eucharist as part of the same process. For example, this emphasis is behind one of the longer alternative confessions, sometimes used in Lent, which contains the following expressions: 'we are truly sorry and repent of all our sins'; 'We have wounded your love and marred your image in us'; and in the second confession in the main text of the Eucharist, we repent with a perspective on past, present and future in these terms: 'in your mercy forgive what we have been, help us to amend what we are, and direct what we shall be'. This is also why we intercede and pray for all manner of concerns, local and national, because the covenant community is located in a particular place and at a particular time and its renewal is about directing discipleship into the surprisingly new ways of God, where we are and where we might be. And it is also about the Peace, however it is shared. The covenant community are bound together, welcoming the newcomer, being reconciled with an enemy, or expressing love for someone known a long time.

Covenant is about binding together and it is the Eucharist's task to renew it, hence the command to repeat, because of the *need* to repeat. The perspective of those seventeenth-century Anglican writers can also help us to see what baptism and eucharist are really for. Richard Hooker put it even more succinctly: 'The grace which we have by the holy Eucharist doth not begin but continue life.'[5] It is baptism which begins and the Eucharist which continues our sacramental life in Christ's covenant of grace. If we start trying to repeat baptism in any way, we are turning baptism into something other than it is intended to be. There are welcome signs of a far greater attention being paid to baptism in our own time than for many years, some would even say centuries. When, for example, I preside at confirmation liturgies, there is nearly always at least one person who has to be baptized; and after the baptism I usually ask the other candidates to come up and dip a finger in the water, in order to mark their foreheads with the sign of the cross, as an expression of the baptismal promises which they have just renewed. It is very eloquent – and it is enough. If we go much further down that road, we run the risk of consumerizing baptism into a renewal or a reaffirmation which we make here, there and everywhere. It is baptism's task to help us to *enter* the covenant. It is the Eucharist's task to *renew* it. Architecture can usefully help, especially when the font is near the entrance and gets in the way of our entry, posing an obstacle rather than being conveniently placed somewhere else.

Betrayal and reconciliation

The Eucharist does not belong to the Church like a piece of private property. It is therefore salutary sometimes for the Church to see itself through the eyes of the society in which it lives. A good example of this is the opera by the British composer Harrison Birtwhistle called *The Last Supper*. Birtwhistle is cagey about his own religious beliefs, but is clearly captivated by the drama of the Last Supper and the power of its meaning in the life of the human race. The music is characteristically haunting and unitive in style, with the occasional motif from plainchant. The libretto was put together by the American poet Robin Blaser, who uses many different sources, from Thomas Traherne to Charles Olson.

The drama consists of the disciples gathering again, one by one, after two thousand years, at the invitation of Ghost, a female figure. They all appear, each with their own characteristics carefully gleaned from the New Testament. After the eleven, Judas appears and is rejected by the others. The central theme of the opera – betrayal – is now explored. Was he the only one to betray Jesus? Suddenly Jesus himself appears, almost unnoticed, and accepts each one of them, with all their failings. He then washes their feet – the grime of two thousand years – beginning with Peter and (shockingly) ending with Judas, who (shockingly) is received back into the fellowship. The meal is then shared – by all. And they depart, one by one. A tableau above the stage draws us through the main events of the passion, starting with the crucifixion and working backwards. The final words, offstage, are by Christ – 'Whom do you seek?' And a cock crows, suggesting Peter's culpability, and our own.

The opera is no eucharist. But it is a startlingly contemporary reminder that the Eucharist is about memorial, remembrance, covenant, cost and sacrifice. For behind all these dynamics of grace there is the fundamental human dynamic of weakness and sin – our betrayal of Christ, which cannot easily be scapegoated into Somebody Else's Problem. And the point suggested by the opera, and made explicit in the Eucharist, is that we betray again and again but we can be forgiven. That is, if we forgive ourselves – and one another, in the way that the disciples had to accept Judas back into their midst. The grime of the centuries ('the Holocaust shattered my heart' is a particularly poignant line) has to be washed away, and then we can sit down to eat and drink. And then the whole process begins all over again.

> Father, we plead with confidence
> his sacrifice made once for all upon the cross;
> we remember his dying and rising in glory,
> and we rejoice that he intercedes for us at your right
> hand.

These are the words which follow the narrative of the institution in Eucharistic Prayer G. Like the other prayers, it fixes on the notion of remembrance and it faces head-on the paradox of the Eucharist, which is that the cross is once and for all, not to be repeated in any way by our efforts, and yet its consequences are being real, here and now. Christ offered himself eternally, and we offer the Eucharist in history. Or, as Michael Ramsey once wrote: 'God in Christ offers; the Church His Body beholds the offering in all its costliness, and is drawn into it.'[6] The Eucharist is about more than remembering a past event, and about more than asking for a nice future. The cross is at its centre, and that is why writers such as Simon Patrick in the seventeenth century and the Scots Presbyterian William Milligan in the nineteenth, who have tried to grapple with the traditional Catholic–Protestant divide, have often had recourse to that word 'plead'; it both recalls and asks at one and the same time; it looks back and it looks forward.[7] And that is what *this* 'remembrance' is fundamentally about. Augustine of Hippo rightly places the eucharistic offering in the context of the worship of the redeemed city:

> The whole redeemed city itself, that is the congregation and society of the saints, is offered as a universal sacrifice to God through the High Priest, who offered Himself in suffering for us in the form of a servant, that we might be the body of so great a Head. . . . This is the sacrifice of Christians, 'the many one body in Christ', which also the Church celebrates in the sacrament of the altar, familiar to the faithful, where it is shown to her that in this thing which she offers she herself is offered.[8]

7 PRESENCE

Mystery

Each performance of a dramatic text or musical score is a critique in the most vital sense of the term: it is an act of penetrative response which makes sense sensible.

To learn by heart is to afford the text or the music an indwelling clarity and life force.

A cultivation of trained, shared remembrance sets a society in natural touch with its own past.[1]

These observations come from the pen of George Steiner, a contemporary writer who stands on the borderlands of philosophy, science and religion. Although he may not like the description, thoughts such as these come across as indications of a 'religious agnosticism', especially as the book, which is called *Real Presences*, ends by placing the activity of the human race on Saturday, between the death of the day before and the rebirth of the day after. Real presence, it would seem, is not the personal property of the Christian Church, for all that Steiner has borrowed the term from the repertoire of eucharistic in-talk.

But that is another way of looking at the Eucharist from all these perspectives. It is, as the first quotation suggests, a critique of the world we live in and the shared values we strive to live by, whether these are (broadly) the consensus of a liberal democracy struggling through a time of radical change, or (narrowly) the Christian Church struggling to handle its past as we move in similar fashion into an uncertain future in a world in which 'spirituality' is much sought after but the organized, historic Church has still a great deal to answer for. New liturgies provide many alternative texts but many of us still want to know at least some of our texts by heart, because the power of the familiar text transcends any local desire to experiment for its own sake. And yet we still want the freedom to adapt, because the 'real presence' of Christ at the end of the day cannot be neatly located, as if our religion could be packaged like goods in a supermarket.

Christ's concluding words in Matthew's Gospel, after all, provide us with a scene in which we are commanded to go out – but with the promise of his presence until the end of time (Matt. 28.18–20). Matthew, sometimes called 'the teacher's Gospel' on account of the large amount of teaching within its bounds, central to which is the Sermon on the Mount, begins by describing the coming saviour in terms of an abiding presence, Emmanuel, God with us (Matt. 1.23). The 'shared remembrance' of Christ's presence is the mainspring of the Church, whether this be in the word narrated in the Gospel or shared in the sermon, or in the sacrament narrated in the eucharistic prayer or shared in communion. There is an abiding presence, not always obvious, not invariably clear, but always there. Even when felt to be absent – and the sense of an absent God is a vital part of the experience of many who strive for faith, especially at difficult times – such a presence is known to be a reality.

This brings us to the word 'mystery', which has been more common in the Christian East than in the West when referring to the Eucharist. 'These holy mysteries' appears in the Post Communion Prayer in the 'traditional' form of the liturgy and it is a survival from the old Prayer Book. But although it makes this sole appearance, it can be read between the lines of the rest of the service as well. Mystery is a way of saying that we do not fully understand what it is that we are experiencing or talking about, but nonetheless we know it to be real and not false. It is not about trying to evade important questions as to how or why or what. The how of the Eucharist is the basic fact of being gathered in the Lord's Name to do his will, with sacred speech and bread and wine. The why of the Eucharist is the life force of the cross in our midst, known in the narrative of our faith but also experienced in the lives we lead. The what of the Eucharist is the equipment of word and the sacred elements, within the changing cultural context in which we happen to find ourselves – a context that happens to have placed us in a community which is now using this particular liturgy. Those questions – and many more which spring from them – will continue to be part of this 'mysterious' life that we share. And that is why the distinction is sometimes made between 'the mystery of the Eucharist' as a reality in its own right and 'the holy mysteries' of the bread and wine which we share. One of the seventeenth-century Anglican divines, Jeremy Taylor, loved to use the language of mystery when speaking of the Eucharist, aware as he was of the many questions people have:

> The holy Communion, or Supper of the Lord is the most sacred, mysterious and useful conjugation of secret and holy things and duties in the Religion. It is not easy to be understood, it is not lightly to be received: it is not much opened to us in the writings of the New Testament, but still left in its mysterious nature.[2]

Taylor, who wrote more about the Eucharist than almost any of his contemporaries, has an important point. Michael

Ramsey, even more influenced by the Eastern Fathers than Taylor, puts it even more directly:

> *Mystery* means that Christ by His body and His blood feeds His people with Himself, and that presence of His body and His blood is not the result of the individual's faith, but, like the Incarnation itself, a presence which faith may receive and which unfaith may reject.[3]

That reference to 'unfaith' may well be an echo of Ramsey's deep distress at the atheism of his brother Frank.

Holy Communion and Holy Spirit

How do these realities find expression in the liturgical texts that we use? Once again, repetition comes to our aid. In every narrative of the institution, Jesus indeed says of the bread, 'this is my body', and he says of the wine, 'this is my blood'. But it is in the words surrounding the narrative that a fuller treatment is given. The narrative on its own is not sufficient, even though there have been times in history when there were those who, usually impatient about historic or seemingly lengthy prayers, wanted to strip the service right down so that almost all that was left was the narrative and nothing else. The place to look for that fuller treatment is where the eucharistic prayer prays for the Holy Spirit to consecrate or bless both the gifts and the communicants, a term that is often referred to as the 'epiclesis', a Greek word meaning 'calling upon'. In some prayers, these two items are separate, with the epiclesis on the gifts coming before the narrative (as in Eucharistic Prayers A, B, C, and E, and in much of the Western tradition), whereas in others they come together (as in D, F, G and H, and in most of the Eastern tradition).[4] The epiclesis of the Holy Spirit is an important aspect of Eastern theology, and it is good that it has made a gradual appearance in the West; for example,

John Henry Newman, while still an Anglican, lamented its absence from the Prayer Book rite, although it had been introduced in its Eastern position in the 1764 Scottish Liturgy.

So, for example, Prayer A prays for the consecration of the gifts before the narrative: 'as we follow his example and obey his command, grant that by the power of your Holy Spirit these gifts of bread and wine may be to us his body and his blood'. And after the narrative it prays that 'as we eat and drink these holy gifts in the presence of your divine majesty, renew us by your Spirit, inspire us with your love, and unite us in the body of your Son, Jesus Christ our Lord.' In Prayer F, the two occur together, after the narrative: 'As we recall the one, perfect sacrifice of our redemption, Father, by your Holy Spirit let these gifts of your creation be to us the body and blood of our Lord Jesus Christ; form us into the likeness of Christ and make us a perfect offering in your sight.'

As far as content is concerned, the two texts (and the others like them) are making what amounts to the same prayer, which is that the bread and wine may be 'to us' the body and blood of Christ, and that by eating and drinking this food and drink in this way, we may be renewed, inspired and united (Prayer A), or formed into Christ's likeness and made a perfect offering (Prayer F). The key point of difference is that whereas all the eucharistic prayers pray for the consecration of the *gifts* in the same kind of words (that the gifts may be 'to us' Christ's body and blood), the ways in which the fruits of *communion* are prayed for vary. Prayer B speaks of being 'gathered into one in your kingdom . . . so that we, in the company of all the saints may praise and glorify you for ever'; Prayer C, resonating Prayer Book language, asks that 'we and all your Church may receive forgiveness of our sins and all other benefits of his passion';

Prayer D prays that 'we may feed on Christ with opened eyes and hearts on fire'; Prayer E asks that we may be helped 'to work together for that day when your kingdom comes and justice and mercy will be seen in all the earth'; Prayer G prays that 'as we eat and drink these holy things in your presence, form us in the likeness of Christ, and build us into a living temple to your glory'; and Prayer H asks, 'make us one in Christ, our risen Lord'.

These variations do not suggest a Church that cannot make up its mind. They suggest that what the Eucharist means is both indefinable and not easy to pin down as to what it is expected to do for us. That need hardly be a surprise, because the Eucharist is at the heart of the gospel community's life. It is about following Christ. It is about being renewed. It is about living lives of praise. It is about being forgiven. It is about having open eyes and hearts on fire. It is about working for the kingdom. It is about being formed into Christ. It is about being built into a living temple. It is about being one in Christ. And it is about much else. The possibilities are inexhaustible and that is how it should be. It is a mystery, a reality into which we are continually growing. Indeed, some of the prayers suggest the language of mystery, as in Prayer A's reference to 'the presence of your divine majesty' and Prayer G's concluding reference to 'the vision of that eternal splendour for which you have created us'.

But public liturgy has to walk steadily between the florid prose of devotional literature and the extensive and analytical language of the doctrinal theologian. For example, one of the matters on which Christians have been divided is how Christ's presence at the Eucharist should be expressed. The two main approaches have tended to be a 'spiritual' view of the presence and a 'physical' view. At the Reformation, the former took over, because the latter tendency was seen by many in the various churches of the Reformation as having been too dominant, with the increasing use of the twelfth-century term 'transubstantiation'. But you will never find that term in an official prayer of any church, even among those who espouse its use. As usual, Richard Hooker strikes a constructive balance:

> Christ assisting this heavenly banquet with his personal and true presence doth by his own divine power add to the natural substance thereof supernatural efficacy, which addition to the nature of those consecrated elements changeth them and maketh them that unto us which otherwise they could not be . . . there ensueth a kind of transubstantiation in us, a true change of body and soul, an alteration from death to life.[5]

Few would dare to say that this expresses a weak or inadequate teaching about the Eucharist. It comes near to saying exactly what the new eucharistic prayers ask: that the gifts be consecrated and that they be received faithfully. Hooker also brings out an emphasis which is notable in much Anglican writing on the Eucharist, that it is at root an action of Christ in his Church. This means that when we come to the ecumenical statements on the Eucharist in our own time, there is something of a balance which is entirely consonant with the 'for us' language of the new eucharistic prayers; indeed, these words are exactly what we find in the old Roman Canon (Roman Eucharistic Prayer I), which goes back many centuries, and significantly speaks of the consecration of bread and wine as 'for us' (the Latin word is 'nobis'). The Anglican–Roman Catholic International Commission's 'Statement' on the Eucharist was something of a breakthrough when it spoke in the following terms: 'The real presence of [Christ's] body and blood can . . . only be understood within the context of the redemptive activity whereby he gives himself, and in himself reconciliation, peace and life, to his own.'[6]

Bread and wine

This brings us to the question of the bread and wine. In no way the fare of the wealthy in the ancient world, it is vegetarian food, simple food, the bread and wine from Jewish sabbath meals, as well as the Passover. But it is more than that. In times past, there have been those who have written about the Eucharist as if there were a great wedge driven between the sacrificial aspect of the Lord's Supper and the presence of Christ at the banquet. But that is to skew things badly. First of all, the bread and wine are themselves the result of crushed corn baked with or without leaven (the Eastern churches and many churches of the Reformation use 'ordinary' bread, whereas the Roman church, in company with many Anglicans and Lutherans, use wafer bread), and crushed grape which is then fermented. The very processes which go into the production of these basic elements are about death and resurrection in the natural world as this is stewarded (baked and fermented!) by human labour. This explains why, for example, words are sometimes used at the presentation of the gifts of bread and wine which try to express both that process – human labour – and at the same time point towards the new use to which the elements are going to be put. Some of the Table Prayers are intended to say this when the bread and wine are presented. But there are echoes elsewhere, in the eucharistic prayers, of the way in which the elements are brought and presented in remembrance of Christ, as food and drink to be eaten and drunk in remembrance of his one offering, eternally made by him and graciously recalled by us. There is a long tradition in both East and West of saying, 'remembering . . . , we offer', because the bread and wine are presented *for God to consecrate them*. Far from the offering of the gifts being an emphasis on 'what we can do', it is a bold statement of our total dependence upon 'what God can do'. Bringing God's gifts of bread and wine before him in the new context of the Eucharist is a profoundly Christian action.

That dependence finds an echo in many writings down the ages. George Herbert expresses it with clarity and depth in a poem entitled 'The Holy Communion', the first two and last stanzas of which are as follows:

> O gracious Lord, how shall I know
> Whether in these gifts thou be so
>   As thou art everywhere;
> Or rather so, as thou alone
> Tak'st all the Lodging, leaving none
>   For thy poor creature there?

> First I am sure, whether bread stay
> Or whether Bread do fly away
>   Concerneth bread, not me.
> But that both thou and all thy train
> Be there, to thy truth, and my gain
>   Concerneth me and Thee. . . .

> This gift of all gifts is the best,
> Thy flesh the least that I request.
>   Thou took'st that pledge from me:
> Give me not that I had before,
> Or give me that, so I have more;
>   My God, give me all Thee.[7]

8 KINGDOM

Past, present and future

Christ has died. Christ is risen. Christ will come again.

These ten words are deceptively straightforward. They have been said or sung in one form or another for many centuries. In the Eastern churches, there has long been the custom of small interjections – either by the deacon or the whole congregation – at various points in the eucharistic prayer. In recent years, this custom has been revived and adapted and this particular acclamation usually comes either immediately after the narrative of the institution or slightly later. They are a form of summary of what the Eucharist is saying and doing.

The words carry a heavy load, for they point the Eucharist in three significant directions. They thus become one of the ways in which the Eucharist is shown to be located in history in the very human context of the particular occasion, whether it is someone's bedside or a great cathedral, and also part of the eternal work of Christ. To say that Christ has died is a historical statement with which even an atheist will agree, for we have incontestable evidence that Jesus of Nazareth was executed at the time of Pontius Pilate – a fact which may explain why his is the only name mentioned in the Creed, apart from the Virgin Mary and Jesus himself. The Christian faith is about a death, and a death is where we begin. But the death is not the end, hence the power of that present-tense assertion that Christ is risen. Here we move from the hard facts of history to the language of faith. We do not say exactly *how* he is risen, what form that resurrection life takes. But without the resurrection, there can be no Christian faith, as Paul points out to the Corinthians in a passage where even he refrains from precise definition (1 Cor. 15.13).

But it is the third statement – 'Christ will come again' – which takes the movement forward. We have looked to the past. We recognize the present. But what of the future? The age of the Internet alerts us to the possibilities as well as the limitations of the future. To be in contact with someone living on the other side of the world, a process which even a century ago took many weeks, can now happen with the press of a button. A shrinking world, however, is a world which still needs redemption, and globalization often serves to show what little power we actually have. The future is not really under our control at all. It is uncertain, it is threatening and it can be very fearful. In what sense can the Eucharist look to the future?

The answer is that it boldly proclaims that it *can* look to the future, and with hope. That is why a number of the eucharistic prayers (A, B, E and F) contain references to the coming of Christ's kingdom regardless of which acclamation is used. The future may not be quite what we want or would like but it is fundamentally God's future. Christ is no mere option among many in the religious market-place. He is the Lord of history. The resurrection is not a historical event like his death, which can be chronicled. The resurrection is a present reality; and because it is a present reality, Christ's 'coming' is an ever-present experience. His 'coming' will be different in the various stages of both our lives and the lives of the communities and nations to which we belong. And our response to those 'comings' will take different forms, sometimes creative, sometimes negative. That mixture of opportunities taken or rejected – or half-taken – will inevitably form much of the substance of our lives and will depend on circumstance. But the Christian faith nonetheless holds on to belief in a God who walks ahead of us: 'keep us firm in the hope you have set before us', as one of the main Post Communion Prayers puts it.

But it is not just the past, the present and the future which are brought together in the Eucharist in this way. It is not just the events of Jesus' ministry, his death and resurrection. Nor is it just our little gathering, huddled together against a sometimes indifferent or hostile world, hoping that somehow things will get better in the future. The Eucharist is one of the principal means of claiming a place in the whole sweep of eternity at work among us now. To look for Christ's 'coming' is about all the future 'comings' that we may experience, whether we are conscious of them or not. And it is also about the final 'coming' at the end of time, vividly described in parts of the New Testament (e.g. 2 Thess. 5.1–11), and also expressed in many well-known hymns (e.g. the anonymous 'Jerusalem, my happy home').

There is, however, one more aspect of this important truth, the link between time and eternity, the union of heaven and earth. It concerns the fact that the Eucharist is far more than the gathering of people who happen to be present on a particular occasion. There are times when the Church is criticized for being too inward looking, too concerned with local issues, perhaps even too cosy with our own little world, and insufficiently conscious of the reality of the communion of saints. Thankfully, the new liturgical calendars have helped redress that balance. There is now a rich provision for exploring the range of people who either have to be commemorated, or may be, whether these are apostles about whom we know little, like Philip and James, or significant holy people about whom (thanks to their writings) we know much more, like Mother Julian of Norwich. Sometimes at a sung celebration, when the congregational setting of the music uses the same themes, the acclamation 'Christ has died . . .' resembles closely what we have earlier sung in the Sanctus, 'Holy, Holy, Holy . . . Heaven and earth are full of your glory . . .' The union of earth and heaven rescues us from an unhelpful inwardness and enables us to realize that the world is a bigger place than we may ever know. In words attributed to Christopher Columbus, 'life has more imagination than we carry in our dreams'. Charles Wesley puts this truth eloquently in one of his many eucharistic hymns:

> How glorious is the life above,
>   Which in this ordinance we taste;
> That fullness of celestial love,
>   That joy which shall for ever last.[1]

The heavenly offering

One particular image must claim our attention when we look at how the union of earth and heaven is expressed in the Eucharist. So far it could be seen as no more than poetry or the sense of the transcendent in an old building, important as both experiences continue to be for many people, not just Christians. The keystone in this arch is Christ himself and the image that has been constantly used to express this part of his ministry is that of heavenly intercession. Three of the eucharistic prayers explicitly refer to this: 'accept through him our great high priest' (A), 'For he is our great high priest, who has loosed us from our sins and has made us a royal priesthood to you' (C, when there is no proper preface), and – most explicit of all – 'we rejoice that he intercedes for us at your right hand' (G).

What does this image mean? When the author of the Letter to the Hebrews speaks of this heavenly intercession (Heb. 7.23–25), what he means is not that Christ is physically talking to God, gathering up all the prayers of the Church across the ages in some kind of everlasting in-tray. Intercession means 'being there on behalf of' others. This is a way of expressing what Christ is doing now for us and it prevents us from locking Christ into two incompatible compartments, one of which is the cross and the other the 'Coming' at the end of time. The heavenly intercession is a vital image which relates Christ's kingdom, his kingship, with what we are doing now. Jeremy Taylor wrote with rare clarity and beauty about this truth in a famous passage which is worth quoting in full:

It is the greatest solemnity of prayer, the most powerful liturgy and means of impetration in this world. For when Christ was consecrated on the cross and became our high-priest, having reconciled us to God by the death of the cross, He became infinitely gracious in the eyes of God, and was admitted to the celestial and eternal priesthood in heaven; where in the virtue of the cross He intercedes for us, and represents an eternal sacrifice in the heavens on our behalf. That He is a priest in heaven, appears in the large discourses and direct affirmatives of St Paul; that there is no other sacrifice to be offered but that on the cross, it is evident, because 'He hath but once appeared in the end of the world to put away sin by the sacrifice of Himself;' and therefore since it is necessary that He hath something to offer so long as He is a priest, and there is no other sacrifice but that of Himself offered upon the cross; it follows that Christ in heaven perpetually offers and represents that sacrifice to His heavenly Father, and in virtue of that obtains all good things for His Church:

> Now what Christ does in heaven, He hath commanded us to do on earth, that is to represent His death, to commemorate this sacrifice, by humble prayer and thankful record; and by faithful manifestations and joyful eucharist to lay before the eyes of our heavenly Father, so ministering in His priesthood, and doing according to His commandment and His example; the church being the image of heaven, the priest the minister of Christ; the holy table being a copy of the celestial altar, and the eternal sacrifice of the Lamb slain from the beginning of the world being always the same; it bleeds no more after the finishing of it on the cross; but it is wonderfully represented in heaven, and graciously represented here; by Christ's action there, by His commandment here.[2]

Beneath the rich language can be seen a powerful and foundational image for relating the Eucharist to Christ. 'Wonderfully represented in heaven, and graciously represented here; by Christ's action there, by His commandment here' – this is eucharist's dynamic, which is all the time the work of God in Christ but also an action which we ourselves make wilfully and safely in the knowledge that it is right to do – 'by His commandment here'. The command to repeat thus issues directly from the heavenly priesthood of Christ. It is not carried out because it may happen to be a pleasing thing to do. Nor is it carried out because it is a command and all commands have to be obeyed. It is carried out because we are given the grace to do so, the logic to see that it coheres with the new world-view that Christ 'comes' all the time to give us.

The heavenly intercession of Christ brings us back to the

cost of the cross and therefore to the language of sacrifice. There is no repetition of Calvary, as Taylor makes abundantly (and repeatedly) clear. But the Eucharist is an action in its own right, the action of Christ in heaven and of ourselves on earth through him. Many writers who have tried to heal the divisions in the West between Catholics and Protestants have used this image to great advantage. Many of the Early Fathers enjoyed it, too. And it has appeared in hymnody as well; the following is an example, a hymn specially written to sum up a series of lectures on eucharistic theology by Richard Parsons:

> We hail thy presence glorious,
> O Christ our great High Priest,
> O'er sin and death victorious
> At Thy thanksgiving feast;
> As Thou art interceding
> For us in heaven above,
> Thy Church on earth is pleading
> Thy perfect work of love. [3]

Kingdom and costly communion

Emil Nolde was one of the school of German artists who flourished in the early part of the twentieth century and are often called the 'Expressionists'. Looking at some of his paintings it is easy to see why. He and his fellow-artists were keen to make their paintings ooze with feeling and reality. They can sometimes almost leap out of their frames. On one occasion, Nolde was reproached for the harshness of one of his creations – could he not make it softer? 'It is exactly the opposite that I am striving for', he replied. 'Strength and inwardness.'

Nolde's *Last Supper*, painted in 1909, is now in the Royal Museum of Fine Arts in Copenhagen. Years later he wrote of the intense feelings he experienced while working on it:

> I painted and painted hardly knowing whether it was night or day, whether I was a human being or only a painter. I saw the painting when I went to bed, it confronted me during the night, it faced me when I woke up.[4]

It is easy to see why Nolde became so involved in the scene, which certainly epitomizes the 'strength and inwardness' for which he strove. The twelve apostles appear standing up, surrounding Jesus, who is in the centre. Some of them are shadowy figures, but the nearer the centre they are, the clearer their faces become, because Christ is wearing a white tunic with a red coat over it. He holds the cup and the apostles nearest to him appear to want to hold it too, in order to drink. But it is the expressions on their faces which leaves a lasting impression. It is as if the whole air is electric with tension. The cost of what it portrays is what strikes the onlooker with a rare force. Nolde, the most obviously religious of the German Expressionists, is here portraying in art the tensions of the age in which he lived, a civilization which was – in his lifetime – to collapse, not once, but twice. While there is agony on Christ's face, which unlike his tunic is yellow, there is enquiry, sharp enquiry, impatient enquiry, on the faces of the apostles.

The Kingdom of Christ is proclaimed in this spirit of enquiry – and of cost. The words of the liturgy that acclaim his death, his resurrection and his coming again are words that trip easily from the tongue, in one or other of the alternative forms: 'Dying you destroyed our death, rising you restored our life: Lord Jesus, come in glory.' We need these words and there will be occasions when they do trip off the tongue. But they keep pointing us back to ourselves in order to help us see beyond what is familiar to us. The perspectives must always turn outwards, back to the cross (as if we could ever forget it) and forward into the future. Similarly, the Kingdom of Christ is about his presence in heaven on our behalf, and our union with him, through faith, through eucharist – and through loving service. Like any other fine work of art, Nolde's *Last Supper* takes us back, in all its strength and inwardness, to the questions that are still being asked and the cost that has yet to be paid, by us.

Christ's kingdom, epitomized in the Beatitudes (Matt. 5.1–12), is about a world turned upside down. Mary Astell, writing in the early eighteenth century, puts it so simply in what is probably one of the very first published comments on the Eucharist by an Anglican woman: 'Our blessed saviour has set us the brightest pattern of every virtue, and the best thing we can do is to form ourselves upon this most perfect example.'[5] This means that communion costs, because it is about our common life, our living the life of faith, our paltry attempts somehow to follow Christ, confident in the dynamic of tradition that has been given to us and not seeing the past as some kind of limit which has to be surpassed. Communion means looking to the future, confident in the surprises and opportunities which are in store for us. Communion means, too, facing the questions and the pain of our present age in all its confusions. Communion, above all, means union with Christ, who 'always lives to make intercession' (Heb. 7.25).[6]

PART 2

INGREDIENTS

9 APPROACH

Preparation

> Careful devotional preparation before the service is recommended for every communicant.

These are the opening words of the 'General Notes' before the start of the CW Eucharist. They may come as something of a surprise. In recent times we have become used to relying far more on the prayers of the service than previous generations. Perhaps with good reason. After all, we should not confuse private prayer with liturgical prayer. The prayers we may say at home are one thing, what we do in church is another. But many people have tacitly given up on private prayer and this is a very un-Anglican thing to do. Past generations relied heavily on the Prayer Book but they often supplemented this with other forms of devotion, which formed a kind of backdrop against which the liturgy was celebrated. There were forms of prayer to be used during the week before going to church, for the days when people received communion infrequently; and there were prayers to be said quietly while the liturgy went on; and there were, too, prayers to be said after the service. It all made Holy Communion a great event.

Those days have gone and with every change there is a gain and a loss. The gain is that we no longer regard the Eucharist as distant from us in a negative sense. All that careful preparation, together with private confession (as one of the Prayer Book Exhortations recommends), could make Holy Communion seem like a difficult suit of armour into which one had somehow to climb. We have more joyous celebrations now, strong in the Easter faith, instead of the more austere and quiet celebrations, perhaps more strong on the cross of Calvary. But there have been some losses as well. The fashion for aiming at one single Sunday eucharist at which everything possible might happen can build up a sense of weariness. As Rowan Williams has remarked, 'If we are busy and bossy with each other, we are likely to become busy and bossy with God.' There is a widespread desire for stillness and silence in public worship and it is interesting to note how the directions for silence have crept into our official forms of service and the way many people come to appreciate it. When stillness and silence are no longer a regular daily experience for people, the Eucharist is the ideal forum for us to use it fruitfully and to value it deeply.

The Form of Preparation provided is suitably flexible. It can be used by individuals before the service – which is probably going to be its most frequent context. It can be used effectively as the first part of the service, replacing the Prayers of Preparation and the Prayers of Penitence. Or it can be used as a separate service on its own, in which case it can include hymns or psalms and should end with the Peace and the Lord's Prayer. These three different contexts themselves indicate the need to bridge any negative gap between liturgical prayer and our own private prayer. The Church is always at its best when that particular gap is at its narrowest – not when its public liturgies are slick and efficient but when people really own the prayers used in the liturgy, think about them and use them to spill over into other forms of prayer which become creative echoes.

The Form is simple and direct. It begins with the 'Veni creator Spiritus', an ancient hymn to the Holy Spirit, written around the same time as the Collect for Purity and originally sung at Vespers at Pentecost, but often used in medieval England by the priest in the sacristy as he prepared to celebrate mass. It was translated by John Cosin in the early seventeenth century and used at ordination and is the only hymn that appears in the Prayer Book. It can thus claim a particular place here, directing the worshipper towards the Holy Spirit. There then follows an exhortation which calls us to self-examination, echoing Paul's warning to the Corinthians: 'Whoever eats the bread or drinks the cup of the Lord in an unworthy manner will be answerable for the body and blood of the Lord. Examine yourselves, and only then eat of the bread and drink of the cup' (1 Cor. 11.27–28). But we need help with such self-examination, for without it we might indulge in morbid self-denunciation. Four alternatives are provided. The Ten Commandments, which have long had a place in the devotional and ethical life of the Church, direct us first to the reality of God and then to our responsibilities towards other people. The Summary of the Law, for long central to Jewish piety, has a similar direction, reminding us to love our neighbour as ourselves, implying that self-love is part of the movement back to God. The Comfortable Words, which have been part of Anglican piety before Communion from the early Prayer Books, is yet more direct: 'Come to me . . .'; 'God so loved the world . . .'; 'Christ Jesus came into the world . . .'; 'If anyone sins . . .' Finally, the Beatitudes: at first sight, they are the most positive of all and they are also just as demanding. Coming from the start of the Sermon on the Mount (Matt. 5.1–10), they have been part of the Liturgy in the Orthodox churches for centuries (originally as a kind of preparation), and there was an attempt to introduce them at the start of the Prayer Book Eucharist in a projected revision late in the seventeenth century.[1] There follows a time of silence, which is appropriate at this point since one or other of these four biblical statements about the life of faith is central to the Form of Preparation, which in turn ends with the confession and absolution.

'Who comes? To whom does He come? For what purpose does He come?' These are the three questions with which Reginald Somerset Ward, a great spiritual writer of the early twentieth century, begins his suggestions for preparation for Communion.[2] Simon Patrick, who was one of the bishops behind the suggested introduction of the Beatitudes in the Eucharist, sums up part of his discussion about preparation in his *Mensa Mystica* ('The Mystical Table') written in 1660, as follows:

> In brief, prayer and praises, meditation of him, and desires after him, reading and hearing of his holy Word, with such like actions, are of that sort wherein we behold his face, and do more sensibly taste of his goodness, and are both more satisfied with him as the greatest sweetness, and transformed into him as the purest beauty.[3]

Presidency

When the Eucharist begins, there are three dimensions of awareness which emerge, either immediately or gradually. One is the fact that there is a community. Another is that there is someone who presides. And most important of all is that community with president are gathered in order to worship God. It is not a meeting in order to transact business, but a gathering with a purpose that is different from anything else. However hard we may try to make it all look normal, the Eucharist is different from everything else that may go on in our lives. In fact, the word 'president' (in

Greek, *proestōs*) is an ordinary term, first used of the Eucharist by Justin Martyr in the middle of the second century, when he was describing Christian procedures to outsiders in order that they should know what happens as well as realize that Christians were normal, loyal citizens.[4]

Presidency of the Eucharist is a relatively recent term – but it has ancient foundations. It first appeared in official texts of the Church of England in 1971 with the appearance of Holy Communion 'Series 3'. Why? Not just because Justin Martyr uses the word. The Prayer Book uses the term 'priest' but there are occasions when the bishop presides, and there may be several priests present as well as deacons with their functions. The real reason for the revival of this ancient term is that it is more relational: the president has to preside over something, whereas priests are priests regardless of whether they are acting as priests or not. Another reason is to combat gently the use of the word 'leader'. Many people do speak of services being 'led' by a particular person. But even though it may be used by those who perhaps would like to underplay notions of ordained ministry, what 'leadership' does is the reverse – it underscores a particular person's dominance of the act of worship. Presidency is about relationships – with the whole assembly as well as with the other ministers present. As Robert Hovda has written, 'Presiding is a service required by any group of people who have gathered for a common purpose. When that purpose is common prayer in the tradition of people of biblical faith, that meeting is a liturgy.'[5]

Not everyone should preside at the Eucharist. Most churches restrict this function to those who have been ordained and even those churches that do not practise ordination have some way of choosing and recognizing this task. Nor can everyone do everything. An age which is

rightly suspicious of inherited institutional roles sometimes
wants to react so far in the other direction that everything
must be shared in some way. But that is to miss the point.
To preside is about representing the Church in a particular
way, and it says something about the Eucharist being the
heart of the whole Church, universal as well as local. To
restrict its presidency to a particular, ordained person is to
say that the Eucharist 'belongs' to the whole Church, to the
communion of saints; not just my particular favourite
service, but to the Church of the early centuries as well as
the Church of the ages to come.

In the General Notes before the CW Eucharist, there is a
fruitful section on 'Ministries', which rightly begins with
the statement that 'Holy Communion is celebrated by the
whole people of God gathered for worship'. It then men-
tions other ministries than that of the whole assembly: the
deacon may bring in the Book of the Gospels, introduce
the confession, read the Gospel itself, preach (if licensed to
do so), take part in the intercessions, prepare the table at
the offertory, take part in the distribution of communion,
as well as in the ablutions of the vessels after communion
and the dismissal. Some of these functions may also be
taken by a Reader, a suggestion which will be followed by
some and rejected by others. But 'the unity of the liturgy is
served by the ministry of the president, who in presiding
over the whole service holds word and sacrament together
and draws the congregation into a worshipping community'.

And it goes on to specify how this is worked out:

The president at Holy Communion . . . expresses this
ministry by saying the opening Greeting, the Absolution,
the Collect, the Peace and the Blessing. The president
must say the Eucharistic Prayer, break the consecrated
bread and receive the sacrament on every occasion.

When appropriate, the president may, after greeting the people, delegate the leadership of all or parts of the Gathering and the Liturgy of the Word to a deacon, Reader or other authorized lay person.

The sweep of these directions is clear. The community is the celebrant. There are other ministries, including those of the deacon and the Reader. The president, however, must express their ministry by performing certain restricted functions, those which define the character of the assembly. It is not about a particular person's rank. It is about giving honour to the whole assembly. It is therefore confusing when presidency of the first part of the service is given over to someone else. This does harm to the unity of Word and Sacrament and it can also give confusing signals to the character of the whole liturgy. In some churches, 'concelebration' is practised, usually following the way this is done in the Roman Catholic Church. 'Concelebration' is meant to express the unity of the different orders within the Church with the bishop. The priests, therefore, gather round the altar, taking care not to perform any of the functions of others, like reading the Gospel if there is a deacon present. The Eastern churches have different and less restrictive forms of concelebration, but this particular way expresses a sense of unity among the priests with their bishop. It is not intended to build up an unnecessary divide between the ordained and the not-ordained, and the spirit in which it is carried out needs, therefore, to take the essential unity of the assembly, under its president, to heart. The gestures of the president express this function. Hands turned towards the congregation indicate a greeting, whereas hands outstretched with palms turned slightly upwards indicate that prayer is being offered on their behalf; and hands stretched over the congregation (or the eucharistic gifts), with or without the sign of the cross, indicate a blessing.

The president's initial task is to greet the people. There are few bolder statements with which to open an assembly than 'The Lord be with you', or 'Grace, mercy and peace from God our Father and the Lord Jesus Christ be with you' or the Easter greeting, 'Alleluia. Christ is risen.' These greetings need no supplementaries. For that reason, and for that reason alone, secular greetings such as 'Good morning' only serve to dumb down the Eucharist, as if the president were the compere at some sort of chat-show, patronizing the rest of the community. Aidan Kavanagh puts it best:

Since one would prefer not to entertain the possibility that the secular greeting is a mark of clerical condescension to the simple and untutored laity, the only alternative is to attribute the secular greeting's use to presidential thoughtlessness of a fairly low order.[6]

Penitence

The Prayers of Penitence are an essential ingredient of the Eucharist. There are occasions, like baptism and ordination, when the demands of the gospel are spelt out in another way. Who is worthy to be baptized or ordained? No one: but by the grace of God alone is this possible. And it is this grace which we claim as forgiven sinners, living thankful lives. The confession of sin is regarded by many as the centre of penitence but the gospel is about forgiveness, which means that the absolution, the declaration of forgiveness, puts the seal on this important preliminary. It is not about endless grovelling. It is about a sober view of ourselves:

By the grace of God given to me I say to everyone among you not to think of yourself more highly than you ought to think, but to think with sober judgement, each according to the measure of faith that God has assigned. (Rom 12.3)

It is in this spirit that we dare to come to confess. There has been some discussion about the most appropriate position for this feature in the Eucharist and there have tended to be two favourites. The Prayer Book has the confession at the start of Morning and Evening Prayer but at the Eucharist places it just before the reception of Communion. The later position in the Prayer Book dates from 1548, when, as a preliminary to the introduction of a fully English service, a vernacular form of confession and absolution in the 'we'-form was inserted into the Latin mass just before receiving the sacrament. And it was in such a later position that it stayed until the recent revisions, the first of which was the Liturgy of the Church of South India (1950). The Roman mass, however, had a form of confession by the priest, in the 'I'-form, which was part of his preparation and came to be said at the altar steps in the Middle Ages. After the Second Vatican Council, this form of confession was revised and became part of virtually every mass, still in its 'I'-form; but there were also short Kyrie forms of confession, which began to be used by other churches as well. The Kyries (Greek for 'Lord, have mercy') were originally part of the Eastern Church's liturgical tradition but came to be used in the Latin West from the sixth century onwards. More mellifluous a sound than the Latin 'miserere nobis', the chanting of 'Kyrie eleison' also has the advantage of indicating that forgiveness is about healing, as the Greek word for 'have mercy' suggests. Eliding this response, originally intended for litanies of intercession, into a form of penitence in this way makes some kind of sense of what might be a bit of liturgical clutter at the start of the Eucharist. But some would prefer not to unravel too much, to have a proper confession, and sing or say the 'Kyries' all the same.

There is also the question of the form in which Prayers of Penitence are to be found. First we are called to confess, then we confess, then the absolution is declared. All three are now variable in form. The invitation may be *ad hoc*, in which case careful preparation is probably a good idea (and favourite themes of the president easily identified by candid friends). There are two main forms of confession, one from *The Alternative Service Book 1980* and the other a new composition, with a happy echo of the Summary of the Law ('we have not loved you with our whole heart . . .'); a focus on past, present and future ('forgive what we have been . . .'); as well as a welcome reference to social responsibility (Micah 6.8). The absolution is the familiar form and, as usual nowadays, allows it to be directed at the congregation ('you' and 'your') or given by the president to everyone ('us' and 'our'), the latter from the Roman rite. The former is the more authentic Anglican way and makes better sense of the reality of absolution. In that connection, we may perhaps lament the contrast between the different forms of absolution randomly available in CW and the clarity of the three in the Prayer Book, where at Morning and Evening Prayer there is a lengthy statement of forgiveness; at the Eucharist, a short declarative prayer; and at Private Confession in the Visitation of the Sick, the more intimate words 'I absolve you'.

All these words matter, because they are about inward realities – our contrition, our desire to turn back to God. They are also about social realities – our need to put things right with others. But at root they are about God's love and forgiveness, which is why they belong in the Eucharist, and why what Lancelot Andrewes described in a sermon on absolution preached while he was still a parish priest in 1600 as 'the embassage of reconciling sinners unto God' is given to the ordained. [7]

10 WORD

Attention

> Listen carefully, my son, to the master's instructions, and
> attend to them with the ear of your heart.[1]

These are the opening words of the Rule of St Benedict, and
they are words that have a value far beyond the religious
communities that will read them regularly as part of their
vocation. Indeed, the revival of interest in the Benedictine
tradition is one of the signs of spiritual life in our times:
there are even abbeys that provide conferences for com-
mercial company managers in order to help them run their
operations more effectively. This is no romanticism, for the
Benedictines left a considerable mark on England in the
Middle Ages, as witness the number of cathedrals like
Durham and Winchester which were also Benedictine
abbeys. The tradition lives on in our own time, not just in
the fact that Durham still treats its bishop like an abbot,
sometimes sitting him in the choir, or that at Winchester
the Cathedral Statutes still contain resonances of the
Benedictine Rule. It lives on in such features of life as, for
example, seeing a bishop's residence or a rectory as a place
of hospitality.

The Liturgy of the Word is a focus for 'listening carefully'
and for 'attending . . . with the ear of your heart'. These
words do not refer to the gathering of information or the

accurate remembering of facts. Were that the case, the best thing we could do would be to send audio-computers to the Eucharist; this would have the advantage of freeing us from the bother of attending altogether, on the pretext that a machine would be able to be there on our behalf and to do the job far better than we could. Accuracy of fact is not what the Liturgy of the Word is about. In a series of ordination retreat addresses some years ago, Mark Santer decided to speak to the candidates about different aspects of the Eucharist and went so far as to describe this part of the liturgy as 'the sacrifice of attention'; he goes on to say:

> Attention to the Word of God is an integral part of every eucharistic celebration. This is no matter of mere liturgical rectitude. The reason why attention to the Word of God is integral to the Eucharist is that it is an essential element of Christian life. How do we listen to the Scriptures in the liturgy? Not as a collection of individuals who happen to be in the same place at the same time thinking any old thoughts that come into our heads. It is as members of a community, as members of the body of which Christ is the head, that we come together to give our common attention to those words and events which have brought us together and have made us into this community . . . We come then to attend and to give ourselves. The attention required of us is in fact a kind of sacrifice.[2]

Sometimes that attention will be partial. There are occasions when the concentration of an individual or a group of people will, for one reason or another, not be total. I can sit and watch a television news bulletin and it goes in one ear and out the other, not because of the content, but because of the time of day, how alert my mind is, and probably also because the format is often very much the same. I don't expect the Liturgy of the Word's format, however, to alter a great deal, because the content is so startlingly different, and because the community of which I am a part is going to vary so much. For example, there may be an occasion when I am in a large gathering listening to a long passage from the Old Testament with which the reader is obviously struggling and we all find ourselves making that bit of an effort to 'attend', and to listen 'with the ear of our heart' to what the passage in its tentative proclamation might be saying to us. Or there may be an occasion when I am in my chapel and the congregation consists of the chaplain and myself; it is early morning at a busy time of year, he is the president, and I am reading a passage from one of the Letters of St John, and even as I then read the words seem to go right over my head. But it doesn't seem to matter. I have attended as far as I am able. And, more important still, I do not always want to be conscious of when God is speaking to me, for there may be a moment later that day or week when what I have read comes back to me. Or there may be a future occasion when the same passage is read by someone else and it speaks to the community with a rare force for which it seemed as if I was being prepared. There can be too much emphasis on the particularities of how we 'learn' about the life of God. It is usually a random process, part of his good providence, and one for which there is only one main recipe for an impatient human race, always so keen to learn everything at once, and that is patience.

This sacrifice of attention has a particular context, built up to by the opening prayers. There is a dramatic focus around the lectern, ambo or pulpit. The president has greeted the congregation, the confession has been said, the Kyrie or the Gloria has been sung. The Collect of the day has been read, neat in style and syntax and the first prayer in the Eucharist so far to be strictly variable for each celebration. Summing up the preparatory part of the Eucharist, it also looks forward to the Word itself, calling us to 'attend. . . with the ear of our hearts'.

Readings

But to what do we attend? The answer is more than a series of readings and a sermon, although that is the sum total in terms of bald 'items' on the liturgical programme. Sometimes this routine character comes across when it seems as if the Word is being skimmed over in order to get to something more important, the eucharistic liturgy, although there are also occasions when the opposite is the case, and the Word seems to be given such a valued place that the Sacrament which follows appears an afterthought. The readings form part of a sequence, leading up to the Gospel. But they are more than just words in a stream. They are a proclamation because they are about the story of the community of which we are a part. In times past there have been those like William Tyndale in the sixteenth century who have given their lives in order that the words of Scripture should be available to everyone regardless of who they are. Tyndale was executed in Antwerp in 1536, having translated the New Testament into English and had it printed in Cologne eleven years earlier. Far more of his simple, pithy prose lives on in the Authorized Version of 1611 than many have realized, which means that he has had a very considerable influence on all English translations of the Bible. The preface to his translation of the New Testament he subsequently revised and published as 'A Pathway into the Holy Scripture', in which the following words appear, redolent of the excitement of the novelty of being able to make the New Testament available for all:

This Evangelion or gospel (that is to say, such joyful tidings) is called the New Testament; because that as a man, when he shall die, appointeth his goods to be dealt and distributed after his death among them which he nameth to be his heirs; even so Christ before his death commanded and appointed that such Evangelion, gospel, or tidings should be declared throughout all the world, and therewith to give unto all that repent and believe, all his goods: that is to say, his life, wherewith he swallowed and devoured up death; his righteousness, wherewith he banished sin; his salvation, wherewith he overcame eternal damnation. Now can the wretched man that knoweth himself to be wrapped in sin, and in danger to death and hell hear no more joyous a thing, than such glad and comfortable tidings of Christ; so that he cannot but be glad, and laugh from the low bottom of his heart, if he believe that the tidings are true.[3]

Tyndale's words have a delightful ring of truth to them, and the fact that we know that they are closely associated not only with the work of translating the Bible but with someone who was to give his life for it, only serves to bring home to us another dimension of the 'sacrifice of attention', namely the cost that can sometimes be required for hearing the words of Christ. But it is one thing is to say that the Bible is there and available, it is another thing to decide how it should be served up for the spiritual consumption of the People of God. Justin Martyr's account of the early Eucharist[4] may have a somewhat matter-of-fact flavour which perhaps was influenced by the fact that he is writing for outsiders. But it is clear that by the fourth century lectionaries had begun to appear, at least for the main seasons of the year. The great centres of church life, Jerusalem, Alexandria, Antioch, Rome and Milan, were

not only in contact with each other but had some influence
on their localities. And although travel was not nearly as
easy as it is for us today, nevertheless we have some
surprises. A nun called Egeria, probably from the Atlantic
coast of France or Spain, visited the Holy Land between the
years 381 and 386 and wrote down what she saw.[5] This
included not only some of the special ceremonies of Holy
Week, like the palm procession and the veneration of the
cross which spread throughout the ancient world. It also
provides some idea of the kind of lection schemes that were
being developed. Comparing what she observes with the
lectionaries used in the following centuries at Jerusalem, it
is clear that there were some basic principles around which
some experimentation and development were taking place.

The basic principles were that the final reading was
invariably the Gospel and there was only one Gospel reading. This was preceded by one or more 'Apostle' readings,
before which came one or more Old Testament readings,
the order being that the Law came before the Prophets.
There is a sense of order about such a sequence. Egeria also
notes the use of psalmody between the readings; there was
a basic core that was sung, presumably because of the need
for familiarity in a constantly changing congregation. As
far as the choice of readings is concerned, Egeria notes, for
example, the reading of the whole of the narrative of the
Presentation of Christ in the Temple at Candlemas, including Anna the prophetess (Luke 2.22–40).

What subsequent centuries do are two things. First of all,
there is a tendency for the readings to reduce in number,
with one from the Old Testament and one from the
Epistles; later the Old Testament begins the drop out as
well. Secondly, there is a tendency to try to cover the whole
of the liturgical year, so that there are set readings for every
Sunday; and with an expanding calendar of saints, there is

an increasing opportunity to use hitherto neglected passage, such as the vision of the four living creatures (Rev.
4.1–11) as the first reading on the feasts of the evangelists,
thanks to the popular symbolism attached to them.[6] The
reduction of eucharistic readings to an Epistle and a Gospel
on most occasions in the early medieval West provided a
basic stability, but it impoverished worshippers, clergy
included, by depriving them of regular exposure to the
great narratives and prophecies of the Old Testament. At
the English Reformation, this was dealt with by retaining
the old eucharistic lectionary in the main, but including Old
Testament readings alongside others from the New
Testament at Morning and Evening Prayer, together with
regular use of the Psalms and Canticles in those two
services.

But we live in different times and in the liturgical ferment
of recent years an entirely new lectionary has been
produced, based around the Eucharist. Originally the
work of Roman Catholic scholars after the Second Vatican
Council, it won acceptance, with some adaptation, among
other churches, first in North America and then elsewhere.
The Revised Common Lectionary is a remarkable consensus and it is this which is now authorized in CW. Its
principles are that the Scriptures should be read in sequence
as far as possible, spread over three years, thus inculcating
a sense of the individual character of each book; each year
majors in one of the first three Gospels but still uses John on
the solemn occasions, another old tradition. This means,
for example, that whereas at the Easter Vigil the Gospel is
the resurrection narrative from Matthew, Mark or Luke,
on Easter morning it is invariably from John. The provision
of psalmody is a welcome development, intended to keep
alive the memory of psalmody in congregations; and the
Alleluia chant serves the purpose of drawing attention to

the unique character of the Gospel reading. There is, however, one major regrettable aspect of the new liturgy here: the specification of chapter and verse, almost universal in Anglican liturgical tradition up to now, has been abandoned in favour of the more austere Roman practice of indicating only the book from which the reading is taken. People need to know *where* they are in what is being read to them from the Scriptures, whether or not they have the text in front of them – which is by no means always the case.

Sermon

The sermon's position in the Eucharist says more about its function than anything else. Relating back to the Gospel, and through that to the other readings, it also points forward to the Creed as the affirmation of the Church's faith, the intercessions as the community's self-offering, and the Peace, the symbol of the unity of the gathering, reconciled in Christ. The preacher thus stands in a relationship with the rest of the Eucharist and those who forget this truth do so at their peril. Similarly, the preacher stands in relationship with the congregation, whether it is a regular appearance of a known figure in the community or a visitor from afar. The Jerusalem practice mentioned by Egeria of several sermons being delivered by a number of presbyters in turn, followed last by the bishop, may startle a modern reader but it is about trying to relate the gospel passage to the particular congregation.

Sometimes the preacher will try to say too much and may forget that, just as only selected passages from Scripture have just been read (and not the whole Bible), so there will be other occasions in the future when other things can be said. As O. C. Edwards remarks at the start of his *Elements of Homiletic*, 'It is much easier to do something if you know in advance what you want to do, if you have some idea of what it looks like when someone does that thing.'[7] This means having a sense of being able to preach and a call by the Church to perform that ministry, which is a heavy responsibility as well as (at times) both an agony and an ecstasy. Preachers will thus have their own memory of other preachers who may have fed them, stimulated them, provoked them, or even bored them. Preachers need to have a clear picture of what they are trying to do and why, and relationships with the community may help or hinder what is being said.

Too much emphasis can be placed on the personality of the preacher and history has its own stories of the cult of the preacher in a locality. Perhaps the emphasis needs to go in the other direction, so that by their style and tone sermons reflect the different aspects not of human personality on its own, but of the nature of the gospel itself. Maribo Cathedral, in south-east Denmark, is a magnificent medieval building with a characteristically grand pulpit, built in 1606, with a large tester above, a vivid sign of the pre-microphone era. There are four panels on the front of the pulpit, each with a particular figure of Jesus teaching the people, each with a one-word Latin description. The first is Matthew's Gospel, and the Latin word underneath is 'terrendo' – the awesome character of Jesus. The second is Mark, whose motto is 'inspirando' – the inspiring character of Jesus. The third is Luke, with 'incitando' – the motivating character of Jesus. And the fourth is John, with 'monendo' – the advising, warning character of Jesus.

We may leave aside the ascription of these aspects of the teaching of Jesus specifically to each one of those evangelists. But we can still heed those four ingredients of preaching – which needs sometimes to be awesome, sometimes inspiring, sometimes to be motivating, and sometimes to warn. And in the various kinds of sermon that can be preached – exegetical, expository, doctrinal, sacramental, devotional and ethical – those four tones need to be registered so that the People of God are nurtured and the eucharistic assembly is left suitably challenged – and hungry for more.

11 CREED

Baptism

A creed is a belief and it is about putting that belief into words. It is not the same as signing a contract, although there is obviously a strong element of commitment. As I grew up I began to learn more about myself and could observe the different ways I behaved towards different people, and so could begin to come to some measure of trust in the relationships that I was forming. I could thus say that I was beginning to 'believe in myself'. And that belief was about many different things, such as the interplay of mind and heart, thought and action. I could trust myself to be able to cross a road or swim, and later on to drive a car. But I couldn't do any of those activities without first learning something about the way and the speed I could walk, the exercise of my arms and legs in water, to say nothing of handling the complexities of a car – and all three involved observing other people.

Something of this growth in faith is perceptible in the way the creeds developed and it is a truism to say that people operate at different speeds, according to their personalities and experiences, as the interaction between Jesus and the apostles indicate in the Gospels. But there is nonetheless a picture of how people expressed their faith and trust in Jesus, as well as the need to put that faith and trust into words. Words do matter, and in matters of faith they require both simplicity and clarity. In the New Testament we have the simple and direct form, 'Jesus is Lord' (1 Cor. 12.3), and there is also a slightly more elaborate form put into the mouth of Philip the eunuch, 'I believe that Jesus Christ is the Son of God', which appears in some manuscripts of Acts 8.37. People confessed their faith when they came to faith. But there was a growing need to put that faith into commonly accepted forms and as time went on, it was inevitable that this should take a trinitarian form, echoing the command to baptize in the threefold name of Father, Son, and Holy Spirit (Matt. 28.19).

It is in the early baptism rites that we find the germs of what is commonly called the Apostles' Creed. And although there are small differences between the rites, it is remarkable how similar they are – including the earliest forms for renouncing the devil. The Apostles' Creed developed directly from the questions asked of the baptismal candidate immediately before being baptized. In *The Apostolic Tradition* of Hippolytus of Rome (early third century), this is the form taken:

> And when the priest takes each one of those who are to receive baptism, he shall bid him renounce, saying:
> I renounce you, Satan, and all your service and all your works. . . .
> And he goes down to the water, let him who baptises lay hands on him saying thus:
> Do you believe in God the Father Almighty?
> And he who is being baptised shall say: I believe.
> Let him forthwith baptise him once, having laid his hand upon him.
> And after this let him say:
> Do you believe in Christ Jesus, the Son of God, who was born from the Holy Spirit from the Virgin Mary, and was

crucified under Pontius Pilate, and died and rose again on the third day alive from the dead, and ascended into heaven, and sits at the right hand of the Father, and will come to judge the living and the dead?
And when he says: I believe, let him be baptised the second time.
And after this let him say:
Do you believe in the Holy Spirit in the Holy Church? And the resurrection of the flesh?
And he who is being baptised shall say: I believe. And so let him be baptised the third time.[1]

Here we have the essence of credal faith in the early centuries of the Church. There were local variations, and it will be noted that there was not yet any formula such as 'I baptise you . . .', because the candidate was washed after each profession of faith. But the main lines of the Apostles' Creed have already been drawn and preceded by the renunciation. The language is simple and clear and the shape is trinitarian. Candidates were taught the Creed and the custom began of making them recite both it and the Lord's Prayer aloud in public on an occasion before the baptism; and when the baptism took place at the Easter Vigil, which became popular in the fourth century, such a recitation of the Creed took place at one of the main services during the weeks immediately preceding. Sometimes more care was taken over them saying the Creed at their baptism than the Lord's Prayer, because they were not going to say the Creed again for themselves, whereas the Lord's Prayer was already in most services.

Something of this close link between baptism and creed has been revived in recent years. Of course it never died and every baptism service has to have a form of public affirmation of faith in it, either by the candidates or by their sponsors. But there is a much stronger emphasis on the baptismal character of the whole Church nowadays than there used to be. When, for example, the Easter Vigil was revived in the Roman Catholic Church in the 1950s, at first there were often no baptism candidates, with the result that a form of renewal of baptismal vows was used by the whole congregation. This practice has spread into many other services and it has given rise to different kinds of affirmation of faith, like those to be found in CW which can be used instead of the Creed in public services and are based on credal material in the New Testament (Phil. 2.6–11; 1 Cor. 15.3–7; Rev. 4.8, 11; 5.9; 22.17, 20, and Eph. 3). They are thus undoubtedly scriptural in tone and content but there needs to be a distinction made between officially authorized creeds and affirmations of faith. It also needs to be clear that the renunciation of evil is an integral part of the baptismal rite and that is one of the features which distinguishes it from the congregation reciting the Creed in the liturgy.

Public collective faith

In all this understandable and welcome baptismal enthusiasm, therefore, a distinction needs to be drawn between what candidates recite at their baptism and what congregations say when they are publicly stating their faith as part of regular worship. As in other respects, there is a case for saying that we have too many of these texts, resulting in the possibility that people will place these shorter, optional affirmations of faith on the same level as the historic creeds. That brings us to another use of credal faith which soon developed in the early centuries – a text agreed by a council of the Church as a document stating what is orthodox faith, whose basic language is not the 'I' of the baptismal candidate but the 'we' of the whole Church. This came at a time when there was a need to hammer out a publicly agreed statement about how Jesus was both God and Man and how the three persons of the Trinity have their being. What is commonly called the 'Nicene' Creed is a version of a creed drawn up and agreed at the Council of Constantinople in 381 but which expresses the faith as agreed at the Council of Nicaea in 325. Similar in structure to the baptismal texts, its language is fuller and it speaks more of the divine nature ('God from God . . .', 'of one Being with the Father . . .').

This creed slowly found its way into the eucharistic liturgy, partly as a test against heresy. It did not travel to the West for the Eucharist until 589, when the Spanish church introduced it. But apart from being translated into Latin, two significant alterations were made which were to give rise to long-lasting difficulties between East and West and persist to this day. First, it was to be no longer 'we' but 'I' – 'credo'. Secondly, because one of the areas of doctrine over which there were difficulties at the time concerned the Holy Spirit, the crucial words 'and the Son' were added to the text after 'who proceeds from the Father', implying that the Holy Spirit proceeds from the Son as well as from the Father. That may seem a small point but it became theological dynamite and while many now regret both these changes, they are part of our inheritance, because this Latin version of the so-called Nicene Creed was gradually introduced elsewhere in the West and eventually became part of the Roman rite in 1014. At the Reformation, the Prayer Books took this version into the Eucharist but followed the Roman custom of using the Apostles' Creed at the daily offices. In the Lutheran churches, however, the Apostles' Creed came to be used often at the Eucharist, as well as its metrical version in hymn-form, written by Luther himself, 'Wir glauben all' an einen Gott'.

Faced with such a complex story and the need in our own time for both variety and simplicity, it comes as no surprise that there is such a rich provision for creeds and affirmations of faith at this stage in the Eucharist. Thanks to the Prayer Book tradition of including the two main creeds in daily worship and (at least theoretically) at every Eucharist, we can be described as one of the most credal churches of all. But it is one thing to say these words frequently and another to try to make sense of such a variety of texts and forms. In the main CW text there is the Nicene Creed in its current modern translation, now restored to 'we' but retaining the phrase 'and the Son' (often referred to by its Latin version *filioque*). Then there is a responsive version of the same text, alternating between president and congregation. This has the advantage of relieving the collective voice of the congregation and it merits more attention than it has received. There follows the same Creed, but with the *filioque* clause omitted, which is why there is the suggestion that it be used 'on suitable ecumenical occasions'. There then comes the Apostles' Creed, in line with Lutheran practice, after which there is the same creed in an interrogatory form as in baptismal usage. After this follows the possibility of using the so-called Athanasian Creed, falsely attributed to the great fourth-century theologian of Alexandria, but more likely the work of a fifth-century writer in Southern France: by far the sharpest and most involved of all the creeds, it has been used in both East and West in connection with the daily offices, which is why the Prayer Book orders it at Mattins on certain holy days. It has largely fallen out of use altogether. There then follow the authorized 'affirmations of faith', among which appears Timothy Dudley-Smith's fine metrical version of the Apostles' Creed, 'We believe in God the Father'.

Clearly, no congregation should go through all these

alternatives on consecutive Sundays! Indeed, it may make some sense to stick to a seasonal pattern, using very few of them. The standard text is the Nicene at the Eucharist, whether said together or responsively. The Apostles' Creed, in whatever form, is the baptismal text and should be used at the Eucharist when there is a baptism. An affirmation of faith may be appropriate on occasions when many children or parents are present who may be unfamiliar with the fuller texts. Although theologically most of these texts cohere, when put together in this way they can give a false impression of hesitancy, when in fact the intention is to reach as many different contexts as possible.

Why creeds at all?

There is a certain irony in having so many texts for a part of the Eucharist which took a thousand years to become part of the main eucharistic liturgy of Western Europe. But it is a false view of developing worship in our own time if we think that we can somehow turn the clock back to some 'pure' and ancient simplicity. We have already observed how there were similarities in the various forms of baptismal profession of faith in antiquity, but nonetheless variations. If you were to travel from one part of Europe to another in the ninth century, you would have encountered some variations in how the Nicene Creed was used at the Eucharist; if you were in Spain, you would hear it recited just before communion, whereas if you were in France, it would come after the Gospel and the sermon (if any), whereas at Rome you would not hear it at all. These un-stable rhythms indicate their own message of tentativeness and they raise the question of what really is the place of officially agreed statements about the Christian faith in the regular worship of the Church.

It is a question that has long been wrestled with. Writing in the middle of the nineteenth century, the great preacher and social reformer F. D. Maurice, who after a Unitarian upbringing became a convinced Anglican and a devotee of the creeds, remarked in a somewhat pragmatic vein that 'the creed has served as a protection to the humbler members of the Church against the inclination which the Church doctors of different ages have manifested to rob them of their inheritance, and to appropriate it to themselves'.[2] (It is the kind of observation he also made in his preaching.) What he is saying is that we need an agreed form and the ancient forms provide a stability around which every kind of person can unite. They are not intellectual statements that are somehow the possession of theologians. They belong to the whole Church and they serve as vital boundary marks which say enough, and permit all of us to think further about what these great truths mean. I cannot expect every single phrase to hit me every time I recite them. But I know that their great words are trying to express the reality of God and the experience of believing in Jesus in a way that has been tested by time.

Wolfhart Pannenberg, one of the great German theologians of the later twentieth century, wrote an exposition of the Apostles' Creed in which he made the following remarks about the nature of trust:

Faith cannot be without an object. In the act of trust a man forsakes himself and anchors himself to the thing or person on which he relies. And consequently, since man cannot live without trust, he is dependent on the truly trustworthy becoming apparent to him. For Isaiah the God of Israel was truly trustworthy; and for the early Christians, who in the words of the Roman baptismal creed repeated their threefold 'I believe', it was the God whose Son had appeared on earth in Jesus Christ and who is present through his Spirit to those who believe in him. The eternal God, who revealed his love for men through Jesus Christ, was for them the unshakeable foundation on which a man can unconditionally build.[3]

It is this personal and collective trust in the truth of God and the inadequate capacity for words to express that trust which underlies the need for creeds. History sets one – the simpler – firmly in the context of baptismal life, and places the other – the more complex – less firmly in the context of eucharistic worship. Our renewed interest in baptism has been one of the reasons for mixing these two traditions together and our desire for variety has provided the rich scope for diversity that is now before us. At the end of the day, it is a question of whether we see the reality of God revealed in Jesus Christ and active in our live in the Holy Spirit or not. If the answer is 'yes', then these historic creeds continue to serve their purpose well. Some modern '*ad hoc*' creeds have been written which are more personal and intuitive in their style and language. They are, in effect, a form of mild protest against the traditional texts but they often fail to express the basic truths of the Trinity and the incarnation.

All these issues raise, too, the question of where the Creed or its alternatives should come and how frequently it should be said. Whatever experience antiquity teaches us about its largely creed-less Eucharist, the great preachers of that era, John Chrysostom and Augustine among them, delivered sermons that flowed naturally into prayer, a tendency that many a preacher knows to be an appropriate conclusion. And with the development of rich hymnody and full eucharistic prayers, there are those who would question the Creed's frequency. The decline of Merbecke's memorable musical setting of the Nicene Creed has also contributed to a less imaginative way of relating to these venerable words, which do sometimes seem more stark when spoken in the modern translation. There is some unsettled business here – but history does not provide as clear an answer as we find elsewhere in the Eucharist.

12 INTERCESSION

Context – our world

On 11 September 2001, the world suddenly became aware of the terrorist attacks in America, and many people are likely in the future to ask themselves, 'Where were you when you heard about it?' I was in my car on my way home, and immediately on arrival I switched on the television. Again and again the central events were described by stunned commentators, fighting for words to describe something that was in every sense shocking. Early the next morning, the Eucharist was celebrated in my chapel for those caught up in the conflict, dead or alive. Interviews on local radio took over, in which I tried both to express the shock and horror we all felt and to cool down any quick reaction which would turn this conflict into a Christianity–Islam war. Portsmouth Cathedral responded swiftly, with a visit to the local mosque that evening, and the issuing of a set of prayers for use throughout the diocese, which I soon discovered had also been relayed to our church schools. As everywhere else, we were all caught up by the sheer enormity of what had happened – 3,000 people killed by suicide pilots – and the sheer distance between our world and God himself. But God has given us the burden of freedom, so we cannot go running to him as an afterthought to put things right as if it is all his fault. And yet his love for us is so immense that he longs to bring us back to himself.

To quote the famous words from the start of Augustine's *Confessions*, 'You have made us for yourself, and our heart is restless until it rests in you.'[1] There are many different kinds of response we can make to that bold claim and there will be occasions of thanksgiving and aspiration when it will be easy to put it into words which we can fully own. But when it is applied to the nuts and bolts of a world which is – to say the least – unsatisfactory, then we are face to face with the question of why we should pray at all about specific things.

There are many calls to prayer in the New Testament, the starkest of which is in the Sermon on the Mount. Jesus warns his followers not to pray in an ostentatious manner, heaping up empty phrases, but instead to be humble in approach and economical in content – which provides him with the platform from which to give us what we call the Lord's Prayer (Matt. 6.9–13). Significantly, what immediately precedes that prayer is the assertion that 'your Father knows what you need before you ask him' (Matt. 6.8), and what immediately follows is the direction that we should forgive as our heavenly Father forgives (Matt. 6.14). The Lord's Prayer itself, so brief in content but so rich in scope, provides a focus which begins with God's nature – the heavenly Father, whose name is hallowed, whose kingdom is coming, and whose will is to be done on earth – and only then moves on to our needs – daily bread for the present, forgiveness for the past, and protection and deliverance in the future. In the (slightly shorter) version of the Lord's Prayer in Luke's Gospel, the disciples first of all ask Jesus to teach them to pray, whereupon the words are given them (Luke 11.2–4), and Jesus immediately exhorts them to put their prayers into practice by lending three loaves of bread to the person who asks for them at a late hour, and telling them to ask, search and knock.[2] For many people, this prayer has been a support in time of trouble as well as a measuring stick by which to assess all other prayers, particularly the intercessions. Indeed, at the Reformation, when set prayers were being criticized as unnecessary, John Calvin's followers in Geneva wrote a lengthy paraphrase on the Lord's Prayer as a sample form of intercession, because the original form – from Jesus himself – was regarded as safe.

The Lord's Prayer is usually part of the intercessions at daily prayer but it does not form part of them at the Eucharist because its more usual position is just before communion, where its well-chosen phrases about the kingdom, daily bread, forgiveness and protection can take on richer meanings. However, it lies between the lines of the intercession because it is the most familiar and the most profound prayer of the Christian – in good times as well as bad. But there is another reason, namely the different contexts in which it is given in the New Testament – the need for forgiveness (Matt. 6.14–15) and to be generous to those in need (Luke 11.5–8). There is a proper response to the nature of prayer, so closely linked to discipleship, which turns the words of prayer into ideals etched on the heart.

The activist, however, may well say that Christianity is therefore the same as doing good and that the prayers we make are purely functional, turning our motivations towards a needy world. To that response must come the rejoinder: prayer is about right attitudes and right words, as we learn in Matthew's Gospel (Matt. 6.5–7), and it is about the disciples asking for right teaching about prayer, as they watch Jesus himself at prayer (Luke 11.1). Prayer is about listening to God, about bending our wills to God (Ps. 119.36), about discerning his purpose for us in the context of a broken and fallen world in need of his love and awaiting his redemption.

Different forms

The intercessions have been expressed in many different forms. Two of the most influential in our own time have different origins. There is the single lengthy prayer, which may have a series of set items into which special petitions are introduced according to the topic of the particular section. The first three forms in CW fall into this category. These repay closer inspection. The first is a series of short petitions, under the headings of Church, nations, local community, suffering, departed and the saints, and it dates back to the Alternative Services Series 2 form of 1966. The second is shorter, covering similar ground but starting with the nations rather than the church and it has its origin in the 'Prayer for All Sorts and Conditions of Men' which first appeared in the 1662 Prayer Book, but with an added petition about the departed and the communion of saints. The third comes from the Prayer Book eucharistic rite and its length and scope give little space for specific petitions.

The other form of intercession is the short litany. It is a frequent item in the Orthodox Liturgy, where the deacon makes a bidding for prayer – 'for . . . let us pray to the Lord' – and this is followed by a response – 'Kyrie, eleison', 'Lord, have mercy'. The earliest texts usually began with a prayer 'for the peace that is from above', echoing Christ's words spoken in the Upper Room about the peace which is not of this world (John 14.27). This particular form is flexible and can be adapted to any number of different situations and it lies behind the other two forms, the first of which is universal in scope, the second giving provision for insertions.

The underlying format of the prayer of intercession, however, appears in the text of the rite. The main topics are listed, not given a set text: the Church of Christ; creation, human society, the sovereign and those in authority; the local community; those who suffer; and the communion of saints.[3] This is a radical departure from the Prayer Book, where there was a set text whose only point of variation was the name of the sovereign, although naming the bishop became common practice in the past century; and there was often a pause after 'those in sorrow, need, sickness, or any kind of adversity' to allow the congregation to remember silently those for whom they would like to pray.

It is important to grasp the full implications of this radical departure and to take stock of a number of issues which it raises, over and above the level of responsibility which it places on those who offer these prayers, particularly at the Sunday Eucharist. First of all, we have travelled from the all-embracing, universal pattern of the Prayer Book to the more particular and focused style of our own era. This has advantages – the prayers of old sometimes seemed to wash over us and we were not always ready to apply them to our own situation. But there are disadvantages too. If our intercessions are so particular, they lose out on the universal dimension of God's nature and love. What we want in our local gathering may imply loss somewhere else, whether it is the weather, the economy, or even a football match success. It is all a question of balance.

Secondly, the local focus can be so particular that it excludes the visitor. For example, the reason why the bishop is named is not because the congregation happens to like him and feels the need to do so. It is because the name of the bishop is a specific statement about that congregation being in communion with him, which is why it comes first among those named in that part of the prayer, regardless of who the church leaders are who follow. But examples of overparticularity result when the intercessor tips the balance far away from issues, so that the personalities dominate. This means that if the intercessor has written the

prayers entirely afresh, perhaps only using the sample
forms as a vague inspiration, then there may be some
real dangers of what might be called 'the hobby-horse
syndrome', with favourite themes and phrases which may
jar and even be predictable.

But the third pitfall is one to which Jack Nicholls draws
attention in a description of the free-for-all intercession
which has, in effect, become the public outpouring of the
private prayers of a particular person.[4] Here we enter the
public outworking of the tension that exists in all intercession between our private requests to God at a particular
moment and the public form which is appropriate for a
large assembly of people: they are not necessarily the same
thing! In some churches, this can work well, whereas in
others it can verge on being embarrassing. I recall a time
when a parishioner was deeply upset about a family problem and it would have been better had they come clean and
withdrawn that particular Sunday; the words that poured
forth may have served as a useful therapy, but they did little
good for the congregation other than alert them to the fact
that one of their number was rather upset.

These are all good problems that have arisen from a
possibility that is fairly new for public worship among
Anglicans. They recall us to the words of Jesus before
giving the Lord's Prayer in the Sermon on the Mount: be
humble in demeanour, short in your words, and aware of
the fact that your heavenly Father knows your needs
already (Matt. 6.5–8). Those three injunctions explain why
the intercessions come at this point in the Eucharist. At
such a mid-point in the service, we have already confessed
our sins and heard the Scriptures read and expounded; and
we have the rest of the service to look forward to, with the
Peace, the setting of the table and the eucharistic meal.
Thus the intercessions are not the liturgical cuckoo at the

ready to take over the eucharistic nest. There is a provisional quality to them and perhaps those who lead them need to heed a warning sometimes given to preachers, which is to remember that there will be other occasions in the future to say some of the things that may have been on the original short-list but were (wisely) discarded in the interests of economy. Few people want the intercessions to end up wilting under a surfeit of *information*. And that may explain why it is good for intercessions to be introduced and concluded in a definite manner, and hence the rich choice of concluding Collects provided in CW, with their God-centred focus.

Issues

The intercession occupies a central role both in the Eucharist and in the life of the worshipper, which means that the overlap between the two is important. In former times, there were devotional manuals which helped bridge the gap, with suggestions on how to apply the big words of the Prayer Book to the smaller issues of local life, which could sometimes loom large, like a local disaster at a colliery or a shipwreck. Nowadays, however, the need is the reverse, to assist locally focused prayers to reach the all-embracing character of the God we love and try to serve. But within that creative tension, there are a number of issues which need to be looked at as well.

The life of prayer echoes the life of the individual and the community in its ups and downs. There will be times when we feel nothing like praying, just as there will be times when the worship of the Church in general and the time of intercession in particular seems lifeless and dry. These are often the occasions when some are tempted to give up but they are usually the times when God is more at work than we realize, in the dryness and dullness, the routines and the apparently meaningless words. This can be compounded by the problem of unanswered prayer, in which the wrestling that we do with life in general seems to be a battle of wills between ourselves and God. A culture that likes to plan everything ahead in detail may have lessons to learn about the life of faith, in which the Virgin Mary's surrender to the Angel Gabriel becomes a pattern, not of shoulder-shrugging resignation in the face of a helpless future, but of a faithful response to a loving God who walks before us – 'Here am I, the servant of the Lord; let it be with me according to your word' (Luke 1.38). As Peter Baelz once wrote, 'Prayer is both a resting in and a wrestling with God'.[5]

For that reason Reginald Somerset Ward's wise words that 'intercession is never made by human beings alone and unaided'[6] provide us with a reminder that intercession is not like trying to pitch an old-fashioned tent that keeps wanting to fall down. Human effort is fallible effort and although we may have something approaching the right attitude and we may have grasped the need to be brief and focused, it is more than likely that we will have forgotten that God knows our needs before we ask them, and that this God in heaven is surrounded by the prayers of the saints (Rev. 8.3–4). That brings us to the question of our awareness of that heavenly dimension, so easily forgotten when the prayers are bald and the intentions seemingly functional, as well as to the question of how we express our relationship with those who have gone before us in the faith. Early Christians never saw the need to divide them up into two water-tight compartments consisting of the departed, who need our prayers to help them get out of purgatory, and the saints, who we can be confident have made it to the heavenly shore; few Roman Catholics would sign up to that caricature view in any case. On the other hand, for many people it is not sufficient simply to say that all we do is give thanks for a life lived on earth and rejoice in the resurrection hope.[7] Prayer is fed by love and knowledge, our love for and knowledge of the person, the cause, the need. While Anglican formularies walk with some circumspection around this issue, many people increasingly find recourse to a simple view, which is that our prayers are united with those before the throne of heaven – the saints, the martyrs, the heroes sung and unsung, and many others who perhaps we would not dream of meeting there one day. As Peter Brett wrote some years ago:

> Prayer is an expression of care. Why should we cease to care because a human body becomes unable to do its job as the embodiment of a person? I have seen many people through the moment of their 'death' and not one was good enough for heaven or bad enough for hell. What a moment for love and care to dry up![8]

Intercession thus stands at a pivotal point not only in the liturgy but in the Christian life. We therefore do it harm by turning it into a stream of words that can sometimes seem like an information bulletin, excluding the outsider (who may even come from a neighbouring parish) and devaluing it from its costly position at the heart of faith to a mere form of superficial activism, which may even cast doubt on what it really means. Dietrich Bonhoeffer, writing prophetically as a young theologian, observed that 'the extent to which a man doubts the value of intercession is the extent to which he is still self-righteous'. [9]

13 PEACE AND OFFERING

Actions and words

> When we have ended the prayers, we greet one another
> with a kiss. Then bread and a cup of mixed wine are
> brought to him who presides over the brethren.[1]

So writes Justin Martyr in the middle of the second century
in Rome, as he explains the teaching and procedures of the
Christian community to an outsider. It is interesting to note
the starkness of what he describes and the swift and matter-
of-fact manner in which what are primarily actions take
place. The kiss is shared and the bread and the cup are
brought to the president. It could well be that Justin's
straight language disguises something more complex, for
we must not assume that the second-century church did
everything very simply. But, on balance, it is likely that he
meant just what he said. There could have been words said
at the greeting and at the presentation of the eucharistic
elements but they probably came later. And came they did,
to the extent that the greeting was covered by the words of
the Peace, which eventually became somewhat stylized and
until recently reserved in the Roman Rite for solemn celebrations; it took place between the ministers only; and it
had been moved centuries before to a position before
Communion. As far as the presentation of the gifts is

concerned, different kinds of prayers came to be written. Some of these were variable, to be used at the conclusion of the presentation just before the eucharistic prayer; others were invariable prayers produced by different regions and served as a kind of devotional backdrop for the celebrant.

Words and actions easily become entangled with each other. A birthday present expresses a relationship between two people but often the giver wants to add something, perhaps in a shy manner, once the gift has been given – 'I wanted to say how much you mean to me.' Or sometimes the gift is trusted as sufficient in itself, a surprise to the receiver which cannot be put into words. The same is true of the greeting of the Peace. We have indeed travelled a long way from the days when the Prayer Book rite concluded with a blessing which began with the words, 'The Peace of God, which passeth all understanding, keep your hearts and minds in the knowledge and love of God, and of his Son Jesus Christ our Lord . . ..' (Phil. 4.7). These are now no longer the only words of peace: we have a greeting as well.

The directions in CW at this point are not quite as simple as Justin's description but they are certainly a good rival (and a definite improvement on the jumble of words and actions which were allowed in ASB Rite A). After the Peace,

A hymn may be sung.

The gifts of the people may be gathered and presented.

The table is prepared and bread and wine are placed upon it.

One or more of the prayers at the preparation of the table may be said.

The president takes the bread and wine.[2]

As we have observed,[3] careful thought needs to be given as to how this whole part of the service – the Peace included – is normally done. What is appropriate in a side-chapel will not work at a Sunday morning celebration, nor will that norm necessarily cover a large-scale occasion like a baptism-confirmation Eucharist. Congregations will need to develop a 'house style' for these kinds of occasions.

Underneath these different styles there are also important points of theology. The Peace is about the nature of the reconciled community – and is a truth that passes both human understanding and the limits of the expression and symbolic potential of even the most flexible liturgy. The presentation of the gifts is about the fact that this bread and this wine have been baked and fermented by the human race and are being set apart from all other bread and wine for a unique sacramental use – and that is a truth that passes both human understanding and all the words and gestures that are deemed appropriate to accompany it, whether they take the form of an *absence* of words and gestures, or whether the gifts and the altar are censed with the perfume of our prayers, and the president then washes his hands as a sign of our unworthiness to approach the throne of grace. Just as some will want to share the Peace with a temperamental reticence, so there are those who will want to present the gifts with a theological reticence. The important truth, however, is that whichever side of the dividing line of reticence we want to occupy, it is clear that, whether we like it or not, we have already entered into a world of symbolism in which the greeting of Peace expresses the truth of that reconciled community and the presentation of the gifts is a conscious and definite action, 'to be set apart from all common uses to this holy use and mystery', as one of the traditional Church of Scotland rites put it.[4] There is a natural tendency to try to drive a wedge between a (simple) functional interpretation, at least of the offertory, and an (elaborate) symbolic interpretation. But this does not really work, for the moment we enter the life of the Eucharist, we have to cope with symbolism – and coping with it does not mean deliberately blinding one's eyes to it.

The Peace

'The Bible has a good share of embracing and kissing', writes Colin Buchanan with his characteristic knack of coming straight to the point.[5] In the Old Testament it is used as a sign of reconciliation after enmity (Gen. 33.4) or after a long parting (Gen. 45.15). But as Buchanan observes, these are not 'liturgical' greetings, although they are solemn and may be described as having the flavour of a ritual greeting about them. In the Gospels, the woman who comes to Jesus when he is eating with the Pharisee anoints and kisses Jesus' feet (Luke 7.36–50), which is easily interpreted as a gesture of love and penitence. But it is in the Epistles that we encounter the holy kiss – and at the end (Rom. 16.16; 1 Cor. 16.20; 2 Cor. 13.12; 1 Thess. 5.26; 1 Pet. 5.14). That may indicate the greeting at the end of the Liturgy of the Word, but there are only a few hints that it is about 'peace' (1 Thess. 5.23 and 1 Pet. 5.14). The use of the Hebrew *Shalom* and its Greek equivalent *Eirēnē* (Matt. 10.13; John 14.27, 20.21) suggest that the greeting of peace and the holy kiss may be different ways of describing the same gesture. The 'wholeness' which this greeting is supposed to convey has many dimensions (love, fellowship, welcome) but underneath it is about the Christian message of reconciliation – hence Jesus' use of this word at his appearance in the Upper Room after the resurrection (John 20.21).

The early centuries provide us with hints of the gradual

appearance of the Peace in the Eucharist. In the *Apostolic Tradition* of Hippolytus, which probably dates from the early third century in Rome, the 'kiss of peace', as it is called, is an integral part of the greeting of the newly consecrated bishop, before he presides at the Eucharist for the first time. But in the next century, Cyril of Jerusalem warns against trivializing this greeting:

> Do not think that *this* kiss ranks with those given in public by common friends. It is not of that sort. *This* kiss blends souls with one another, and solicits for them entire forgiveness. Therefore the kiss is the sign that our souls are mingled together, and have banished all remembrance of wrongs. For this cause Christ said, 'If you bring your gift . . . first be reconciled with your brother, and then come and offer your gift' [Matt. 5.23–24]. The kiss therefore is reconciliation and for this reason holy.[6]

Cyril provides a great deal in this teaching to the newly baptized and confirmed. To those unfamiliar with it, the greeting must have looked very similar to its secular counterpart. But it is its context which makes the difference, as part of the Eucharist and made at the point in the liturgy when the gifts are about to be presented. It may well be that Cyril was not the first to use Jesus' teaching from the Sermon on the Mount (Matt. 5.23–24) to explain the greeting as a sign of reconciliation and unity. But there was an alternative position for the Peace, just before communion, as Augustine explains:

> After the Lord's Prayer is said 'peace be with you': and Christians kiss each other with a holy kiss. The kiss is a sign of peace; just as their lips declare, so let it be morally. That is, as your lips draw near to the lips of your

brother, so your heart must not draw away from his heart.[7]

It seems that this was the position being adopted at Rome, although there is no clear reason given for it except as a sign of unity before receiving communion. In subsequent centuries in the Roman rite the kiss became an embrace and later was only shared among the ministers. In the First Prayer Book of 1549 it survives in verbal form at this point but disappeared altogether in 1552.

Its reappearance was dramatic. This came in the Eucharist of the (United) Church of South India, which first appeared in 1950, where it comes immediately before the presentation of the gifts. Although there is a note of caution (it is optional, and the form of the gesture was at first somewhat stylized), it is nonetheless a landmark, showing the South India Eucharist as the pioneer in liturgical revision that it turned out to be. Thereafter it gradually entered mainstream liturgies, restored in the Roman rite after the Second Vatican Council, though still in the pre-communion position, and introduced into most other liturgies, Anglican included. 'Let us offer one another a sign of peace' is the deacon's call in the Roman mass, implicitly indicating that the precise form of the gesture will vary. And while in CW it is directed to take place in the traditional position, before the presentation of the gifts, it can also take place elsewhere, either before communion (as in Rome) or at the very end (as suggested in the New Testament epistles). There are always Anglicans who will follow the Roman rite if they possibly can but they perhaps need to consider two points: one is the fact that it can be unnecessarily disruptive just before communion; and, secondly, many Roman liturgists think the more ancient position is better.

There remain two significant questions. The first is that there are many different forms for introducing the Peace. They will require careful choice. The second is that in CW the gesture is optional – 'all *may* exchange a sign of peace'. There are people who live in love and charity with one another but who cannot stand the gesture, whatever form it takes. Sometimes it can get badly out of hand, with some people greeting their friends and ignoring others. It can be trivialized, as Cyril of Jerusalem wisely observed. The sacredness of the gesture is marked by its context and its position. But it is something of an irony that at the very point in our own culture where physical gestures in public are increasingly suspect, the Church is the place where it is possible to embrace, shake hands, or kiss on the lips. Norms of expectation are useful: for example, a small group worshipping at a retreat centre may choose to hold hands together, to forestall a free-for-all; whereas on a Sunday morning, what might be a formal mood could be broken for a time of informality. The playwright Alan Bennett describes attending the requiem of an old lady who for fifteen years lived in a van in his garden, and his own feeling as what he describes as 'the affirmation of fellow-ship' neared: 'The old man, who was my neighbour, turned round and shook hands and with such an unselfconscious goodness that I was straight away put to shame and saw how in these circumstances my liturgical fastidiousness was sheer snobbery.'[8]

Offerings

'Nothing in my hand I bring, simply to thy cross I cling' are memorable words from Augustus Toplady's famous hymn, 'Rock of ages, cleft for me'.[9] They express the sentiments of the child of the Reformation, who finds it impossible to speak of any offering other than the once-and-for-all sacrifice of Christ upon the cross. That essential protest is against any language of sacrifice that is not handled carefully, if it is used at all. It was understandable at the Reformation, because the Roman mass had an emphasis on sacrifice in its language that gave it a theological onesidedness; the language of its sole eucharistic prayer at the time (the 'Roman Canon') was focused on sacrifice and offering and easily seen by its Reformation critics as overshadowing the themes of thanksgiving and memorial; and the many offertory prayers that were in use (sometimes referred to as 'the little canon') duplicated some of its language.

The result was that in the first English Prayer Books, there was a counter-reaction and a new emphasis on the offering of money while the offertory sentences were being said. But the ritual placing of the gifts of bread and wine crept back in, as we find in the 1662 Prayer Book, and were given theological interpretation by various writers of that era. The opening words of David's prayer before Solomon's anointing as his successor, 'Yours, Lord . . .' (1 Chron. 29.11), were used as the main basis for restoring some kind of prayer at this point, although commentators varied as to whether it should refer to the offering of money or the eucharistic gifts. That same ambiguity is to be found in the selection of prayers suggested for the preparation of the table. The first is a responsorial form of 'Yours, Lord . . .' and its language and scope can refer either specifically to the bread and the wine or to all the gifts. The second and third are explicitly about money. The fourth is a slight rewriting of the prayers said by the president in the new Roman rite while placing the eucharistic gifts on the altar. The fifth, invoking the presence of Christ, is a prayer originally used in the old Spanish ('Visigothic') rite, and used in the South India liturgy. The sixth is adapted from a prayer in the Early Church *Didache*[10] about the unity of the Church. The remainder have different themes, the last four being unspecific and all-embracing in their content, though pointing forward to the eucharistic feast which is about to start.

The choice is thus considerable and while the strength of this collection of prayers is that they are firmly grouped together, their content varies too much for an overall coherence to be apparent. Prayers specifically about money will be appropriate on those occasions when the service is not a eucharist and consists of the Liturgy of the Word. Prayers which are ambiguous will be appropriate on other occasions. In a stewardship-conscious age it is important that the offerings of the people in the money collected should be presented at the altar. A way through this thicket is to keep a cool head and not try to use too much. The altar is prepared, either from the procession of the gifts or having them brought from the credence table. All this takes place in silence, though the 'Blessed are you' prayers could be used silently (as originally intended in the Roman rite) at a sung celebration or aloud at a said celebration when the president stands at the altar. (The washing of the hands – which needs to be visible – takes place at this point.) The main prayer, however, should be all-embracing and is said aloud at the end of the hymn, by which time the money has been presented – either placed on the altar or (better still) greeted with a bow from the president to those presenting it, after which it is placed somewhere else. The corresponding Prayer Over the Gifts in the Roman rite usually refers explicitly to the bread and the wine, although originally it was often more general in tone and content.

David's prayer was said after giving Solomon the plans for the temple he would in time build, which was set up on a site God told him to choose for that purpose; it was originally the threshing-floor of Araunah the Jebusite (2 Sam. 24.18–25). When David approached Araunah with his request and an offer of compensation, Araunah would have none of it. Araunah's generosity in the face of the commands of God was about to go as far as giving David not only the threshing-floor but the oxen for the sacrifice as well, but the king refused. 'I will not offer burnt-offerings to the Lord my God that cost me nothing' (2 Sam. 24.24). That is an underlying attitude which speaks volumes about the grace and mercy of God, about the need for right relationships, and above all about the location of eucharistic sacrifice in the heart of the community.

14 THE EUCHARISTIC PRAYER

Deep structures

> We give thanks to you, our Father, for the holy vine of
> your child David, which you have made known to us
> through your child Jesus; glory to you for evermore.

> We give thanks to you, our Father, for the life and
> knowledge which you have made known to us through
> your child Jesus; glory to you for evermore.

> As this broken bread was scattered over the mountains,
> and when brought together became one, so let your
> Church be brought together from the ends of the earth
> into your kingdom; for yours are the glory and the power
> through Jesus Christ for evermore.[1]

In this way, some early Christian communities gave thanks
at their eucharist. Taken from an early Christian manual of
church order called the *Didache* (or 'Teaching'), these
prayers probably come from Syria and they show a kinship
with Jewish meal-prayers in the way that they first give
thanks for food and drink and move on to supplication,
asking for the blessing of God on the meal.[2]

Why are these early roots so important for us? The main
reason is that in every generation there needs to be a way of

delving into the past, in order to look again at the tradition
we have inherited. This happens still. New data emerge and
new ways of looking at familiar evidence. The second
reason is even more central. Time and again people have
looked to the origins of Christianity in general and the
Eucharist in particular and have tried to compare what they
see with how things are expressed and carried out in their
own time. For example, at the Reformation there was an
understandable desire to look critically at forms of church
order and worship as these had been inherited from
medieval Catholicism, to prune away what was thought
secondary and 'return' to a more biblical faith. And that
desire lingers on today in a similar desire to 'return' to
Scripture and take the process of Reformation even further.

Central to this quest is what we say and do at the
Eucharist over the bread and cup at this central point in the
service. Words (and to a lesser extent gestures) suddenly
become very important and while one can sympathize with
those who are impatient about details (not everyone has the
stomach for endless debates about the Lord's Supper!), it is
nonetheless worth the effort to persist. In our own time the
rites of the Eucharist in the major churches of the West
have undergone a process of revision which has shown us
just how much we all have in common. Roman Catholics
have learnt, not least through their new eucharistic prayers,
to recover a sense of eucharist as thanksgiving and memorial, not just sacrifice. Protestants have learnt, through a
fuller reading of the Early Fathers, that sacrifice is not a
dirty word and that its early use was about celebrating the
memorial of the passion and the work of the cross in us
now at that Table. There has been for all of us a renewal of
understanding about the work of the Holy Spirit in the
Eucharist, which had always been present in prayers and
hymnody but not nearly as explicitly as now. Of all the

international ecumenical texts, it is perhaps the World
Council of Churches Faith and Order 'Lima' Agreement on
Baptism, Eucharist and Ministry (1982) that reflects these
'deep structures' most fully, with its stress on the Eucharist
as a sacrifice of thanksgiving and supplication.[3]

All this has helped to make Christians today far more
aware of a common tradition and a witness in a different
kind of world, where sharp questions are asked about what
all this really means – and *does* – in today's world in a
sometimes direct manner by those who are either not of the
household of faith or who are on the fringes. One of the
great by-products of the renewed interest in the Jewish
roots of Christian worship[4] is that we have been able to
grasp more fully those deep structures of the eucharistic
prayer – thanksgiving and supplication – as the two fundamental features of the prayer in which the Christian Church
is able to locate in praise and intercession what it wants to
say and ask about at the eucharistic table.

But, of course, it is one thing to recover a significant truth
and another matter to decide as a church exactly how we
should use it. I suppose that across the years I have become
aware of these two basics ways of praying because I want
to thank God for certain things and I want to ask him about
others. When it comes to the eucharistic prayer we are not
in the realm of private devotions or a DIY liturgy. What the
Christian community says about what it believes over that
bread and that cup matters. Some churches will answer that
question by being prescriptive, providing a breadth and
width of official forms of prayer – which is where the
churches of the Anglican Communion stand, in company
with many others, Roman Catholic included. It is only in
the past thirty years that we have become accustomed to
alternative eucharistic prayers. Before that time, the only
point of variety was in the 'preface', the special proclamation

at the start of the prayer, which sometimes varied according to season and occasion.

Our knowledge of the early centuries is more extensive
than that of our forebears at the Reformation. This doesn't
mean that what *we* write is better than what *they* wrote! It
simply places another kind of burden on our shoulders:
How do we use that knowledge in order to fashion new
prayers for our own age? The eucharistic prayers in CW are
the result of an imaginative use of many different kinds of
sources, ancient, Reformation and modern.[5] They all
demonstrate those deep structures of eucharistic prayer,
which is an act of praise and thanksgiving for the central
events and truths of the Christian faith and an act of
supplication and intercession for the working of those
events and truths in the Christian community now. There is
ample scope for variation, some prayers having more of
one than another;[6] for example, the Extended Prefaces give
scope for full thanksgivings, whereas Prayer F recounts
salvation history in an extended style.

Anamnesis and epiclesis: memorial and invocation

When it comes to what we ask for at the Eucharist, there is
considerable scope for detail. That is probably why two
particular terms have emerged as ways of looking at the
second part of the eucharistic prayer – anamnesis and
epiclesis. 'Anamnesis' is the word used by Paul and Luke in
their narratives of the Last Supper, when Jesus gives the
disciples the command to repeat the meal – 'do this for my
remembrance' (1 Cor. 11.26 and Luke 22.19). It not only
covers how we approach what we are doing at the
Eucharist. It has come to be applied to the paragraph that
usually follows the narrative of the supper itself, which
often begins along the lines of 'therefore remembering his

death and resurrection'. This makes a good deal of sense; if the institution narrative is to be part of the prayer, then it needs some words to follow it in order to set it in its wider context. The supper took place in this way, which is why we go on to make the memorial of the cross in this particular eucharistic meal.

But what should go into the anamnesis? The prayers in CW are at one with most other kindred prayers in placing the cross centre-stage, and (in Prayers A, B and C, and F and G) in adding the resurrection and ascension. But the problem comes with what we say about the bread and cup. In one of his sermons, John Chrysostom has this to say:

> We offer every day, making a memorial of his death. This is one sacrifice, not many. And why? Because it was offered once. It resembles in this the sacrifice which was taken into the Holy of Holies . . . Christ is everywhere one, entire in this place and in that, one body . . . and so one sacrifice. . . . We offer the same sacrifice: or rather we make a memorial of that sacrifice.[7]

These words have been carefully weighed. For John Chrysostom, the Eucharist is an offering and in the liturgy attributed to him this is what we find:

> We therefore, remembering this saving commandment and all the things that were done on the cross, the tomb, the resurrection on the third day, the ascension into heaven, the session at the right hand, the second and glorious coming again; offering you your own from your own, in all and for all, we hymn you, we bless you, we give you thanks, Lord, and pray to you our God.[8]

There is no repetition of the cross in Chrysostom's teaching or his prayer. The Eucharist is not a means of limiting the work of Christ. But it is a necessary focus – necessary because as human beings we *need* such a focus, which is exactly what Christ gives the Church. In the anamnesis part of the prayer, some traditions will offer the bread and cup, others will bring them, others again will refer to them as part of the eucharistic action. What is important to understand is that since the bread and cup are essential for the Eucharist, they ought to be referred to explicitly in this part of the prayer, either here or elsewhere.

Then there is epiclesis – invocation. Another Greek word, it means 'calling upon', and was first used in the second century by Irenaeus to speak of calling God's grace upon the elements at the Lord's Supper; Irenaeus was protesting against those who would overspiritualize the Christian belief that earthly things can contain heavenly life. Such an invocation later came to be applied to the consecration of the bread and wine at the Eucharist and also the water at baptism, with specific mention of the Holy Spirit, so reflecting the various liturgical texts that were in use and their commentaries. Because in the Eastern liturgies a stronger emphasis on the work of the Spirit developed in these two sacraments, 'epiclesis' became the term used when speaking of eucharistic consecration completed by the Holy Spirit.

But what about the place and wording of this 'epiclesis'? There is an unresolved disagreement about this question between Rome and Constantinople. It is reflected in the CW Prayers, and it relates to who and what is being consecrated. At one level, the answer is simple: the gifts and the communicants. But the way that these truths are handled has varied. The old Roman 'canon', which has been part of the Roman tradition since the sixth century at least, prays for the consecration of gifts before the narrative of the supper, and then later prays for the consecration of the communicants, and does both without any reference to the Holy Spirit. This arrangement, with the important inclusion of the Holy Spirit in both parts, is what we find in the new eucharistic prayers in the Roman Missal (Prayers 2, 3 and 4). It is also echoed, but with some softening of the theological language, in all four of the eucharistic prayers in *The Alternative Service Book 1980*. But other Anglican Provinces, notably Scotland (from 1764) and the USA (from 1789), chose the position adopted in the early centuries by the majority of the Eastern churches, which is to pray for the Holy Spirit to come on the gifts and the communicants at one and the same time, after the institution narrative and the anamnesis.

The eucharistic prayers in CW do not attempt to resolve this dilemma but reflect it faithfully: some of them follow the 'Western' pattern (A, B, C and E) and others follow the 'Eastern' pattern (D, F, G and H). Such even-handedness may be seen as an Anglican virtue. It is, in fact, where worldwide Christianity stands. The net result is twofold. There is an important choice, but the choice reflects different theological emphases. If you call on the Spirit for the blessing of the gifts *before* the narrative of the supper, then you are pointing to that narrative as having an even greater centrality than it has already by virtue of its scriptural basis as the performative word, accomplishing the Lord's command (Isa. 55.11). If, on the other hand, you pray *after* that narrative for the Spirit to bless the gifts and the faithful at the same time, then you are highlighting the work of the Spirit in whose power we are enabled to pray (Rom. 8.26–27), thereby making the important point that eucharistic consecration is about both the people and the elements: the bread and wine are there to feed the community and the community is there in order to feed faithfully. Epiclesis at its fullest leads, too, into intercession, as in the

prayers of the Eastern churches and the Roman rite, as well
as Prayers F and G in CW, since to pray for the blessing of
the Spirit on the working community is also to pray for its
witness – and for the whole world.

In whatever way the epiclesis is expressed, what these
two movements of prayer – memorial and invocation – do
is to locate the Eucharist in *time*. We look back to the cross
and we look forward to the work of the Spirit. The
Eucharist is thus rescued from being an idea or a theme. It
is an action by the Church. As Lancelot Andrewes says in
his Easter Day 1612 sermon, 'it is not mental thinking, or
verbal speaking: there must be somewhat done, to celebrate
this memory'.[9] But memorial and invocation also locate the
Eucharist in *space*. It is a very physical celebration, as
Irenaeus observed:

> We offer to him what is his own, suitably proclaiming
> the communion and unity of flesh and spirit. For, as the
> bread, which comes from the earth, receives the invoca-
> tion [epiclesis] of God, and then it is no longer common
> bread but Eucharist, consists of two things, an earthly
> and a heavenly; so our bodies, after partaking of the
> Eucharist, are no longer corruptible, having the hope of
> the eternal resurrection.[10]

Response

By now it will have become clear that the eucharistic prayer
is not a simple matter. It is about language, it is about
rhythm, it is about liturgical norms – and it is about theology. And in the face of this rich fare, there grew up a
practice from the early centuries of signalling its uniqueness
in a number of ways.

One is by the opening dialogue, which is a public

conversation between the president and the congregation. Although the precise language has varied slightly, it is remarkably uniform in its overall form from one liturgy to another. (It is to be regretted that the vague and banal alternative, 'The Lord is here', from the 1971 Series 3 text still appears.) After the opening greeting, the congregation is bidden to lift up their hearts, a clear signal of the joyous feast which is about to take place, and to give thanks to the Lord, an equally clear signal that the prayer which follows is 'eucharistic', a prayer of thanksgiving. The chants sometimes used for these words are another indication of the fundamental difference between this particular prayer and all others.

Another way is the use of the Sanctus.[11] Inspired by Jewish worship (Isa. 6.3), especially in the piety which meditated on the unity of heaven and earth, this hymn was used by early Christians (Rev. 4.8). In this position it makes the bold claim that the particular eucharist that is being celebrated is not an isolated event but a drawing of the earthly altar into union with the heavenly. It thus performs the function of being not just a hymn, but a particular hymn, with words that are full of meaning. The Benedictus qui venit, an early addition (Matt. 21.9), was kept in the 1549 Prayer Book but disappeared in 1552, although it has been restored through the influence of musical settings and recent revisions. It serves as an eloquent link between the hymn of praise to the thrice-holy God and the presence of Christ, the One who comes in the name of the Lord, at the eucharistic table.

Yet another way is the use of acclamation. This is another borrowing from the East that reappeared in the South India Liturgy (1950) and was taken up in the Roman rite after the Second Vatican Council. The main acclamations inspired by this tradition ('Christ has died . . .') used to come immediately after the institution narrative, but in Prayer A they now come later, an inconsistency which may have historical parallels but causes unnecessary confusion on the ground. In the East it is also traditional for various interjections to be made all through the prayer, which is an option in several of the CW texts (e.g. 'Amen, Lord, we believe' in Prayer F). Overall, the acclamation is a means of signalling another high point in the course of the prayer – the words at the supper and the memorial of the passion, which is why the texts concerned usually evoke Christ's death and his coming again.

Then there is the use of the doxology, which we also saw in the *Didache* – 'for yours are the power and glory through Jesus Christ for evermore'. To end any prayer with doxology, an ascription of praise, is far more common in the East than in the West, where the tendency is to end solely 'through Jesus Christ our Lord'. To conclude like this rounds off the central prayer of the Eucharist in a manner that draws attention to the whole action as being praise, and the ancient custom of raising the bread and cup at *this* point (not earlier) for all to see expresses the union of praise in the gifts now blessed and about to be shared.

All these 'responses' point to the interactive character of this prayer – whether such interactivity is verbally expressed or silently given. Some enjoy listening to the whole prayer, whether it is said or sung – and it is possible to sing the entirety, as has been the case for centuries in East and West. Others want to participate verbally, hence, for example, the format of Prayer H, which – unlike the others – actually ends with the Sanctus. Congregations need to find some kind of rhythm as to which prayers are used when, and the musical possibilities – particularly in the responses and acclamations – can be explored much further than is often the case, especially – even – in the presence of many children. But the best kind of response within the eucharistic prayer is about more than claiming things to be said or sung by the congregation. It is about exploring and reflecting on the meaning of these rich texts.

EXCURSUS: THE EIGHT EUCHARISTIC PRAYERS

Building bricks

> As everyone knows, we are not content in the liturgy simply to recite the words recorded by St Paul or the Gospels, but we add others words both before and after, words of great importance for this mystery.[1]

This is how Basil of Caesarea, one of the greatest of the fourth-century Greek Fathers, describes why the eucharistic prayer exists at all and he does so in a work which explains why the Holy Spirit is divine and not just an idea or an influence or a nice feeling. Of course the words of Christ are a central focus, and some have gone so far as to regard them as words of consecration. But the rest of the prayer matters too and in our own time we have rediscovered the importance of creation and kingdom as well as the place of the Holy Spirit in the prayer. This is not just because the words sound rich and resonant, but because the beauties and responsibilities of creation, the values and truths of the kingdom of justice and peace, and the dynamic of the Creator Spirit in the life of the community are central to what Christianity is about.

All these truths have to be put into shapes of words, sequences of ideas – a narrative of the gospel itself. There are many ways of describing them. The 'deep structures' of thanks for creation and redemption underlie them and lead on to supplication – asking – for the blessing of God on what we are doing. Then there is the interactive character of the prayer: the opening dialogue, the Sanctus, the acclamation, the concluding doxology – as well as any other responses in the course of the prayer. And there is also the traditional way of looking at the unfolding narrative of the prayer: the dialogue; the preface; the Sanctus; the post-Sanctus; the consecration epiclesis (if it comes here); the institution narrative; the anamnesis (which Karl Rahner, the Roman Catholic theologian, once described as 'the primal, constitutive words of the Church'[2]); the communion epiclesis; the intercessions (if any); and the concluding doxology.

All these terms are approximations, for they can be seen in isolation from each other and can undermine the very unity of the prayer which so much good scholarship, research and liturgical creativity have been trying to bring to the fore. Moreover, the individual character of each prayer needs to be appreciated, even though – as with A, B, C and E – there are variable 'prefaces' which can be used in the first part, and even though – as with A and F and others, if so desired – there are responses which can be used. *All* these words are, in the words of Basil of Caesarea, 'of great importance for this mystery'. They may form patterns and structures and those patterns and structures help to give them shape and coherence, but the success of the prayer – in rhetorical terms – depends to a great extent on the sense of overall unity which it expresses. And the opening dialogue sets the scene, for it is about president *with* congregation, which means both sides of the partnership knowing, cherishing and praying it.[3]

Prayer A

This prayer is probably one of the most familiar in its style
and ethos. Although it is a slightly edited amalgamation of
Prayers 1 and 2 of the ASB, in essence it goes back (*via*
Series 3 in 1971) to the Series 2 liturgy of 1967 and can thus
claim an important place in Church of England liturgical
revision. Although there are differences between ASB 1 and
2, the decision to draw them together was uncontroversial
and, in the event, comparatively unlaborious. Influenced by
the eucharistic prayer of the *Apostolic Tradition* of
Hippolytus (though less so than Prayer B), its strength lies
in the narrative of creation and redemption interwoven
from the start: 'For he is your living Word; through him
you have created all things from the beginning and formed
us in your own image.' 'Born of a woman' (Gal. 4.4) was a
felicitous replacement for the original 'born as man'. In the
post-Sanctus, 'Accept our praises' continues the theme of
thanksgiving and establishes an important point of reference for 'Accept through him, our great high priest' later
on. Like B, C and E, there are two epicleses – one before the
narrative for the consecration of the gifts and one later on
for the communicants. This latter retains the threefold petition in Series 3, 'renew us by your Spirit, inspire us with
your love, and unite us in the body of your Son'. In the
anamnesis, the notion of memorial is carefully set out
through the use of those three strong verbs, 'we remember
. . . we proclaim . . . we look for . . . ', thus echoing some of
the thinking behind the Anglican–Roman Catholic
International Commission's 'Statement' on the Eucharist,
which appeared around the same time as the Series 3 text;
but it is now a long paragraph and at the end reads a little
clumsily. The position of the acclamation *after* the anamnesis is likely to confuse congregations who use this prayer

alongside Prayer B, where the acclamation comes immediately after the institution narrative.

Prayer B

This prayer dates back to 1978, when – just before the appearance of the ASB two years later – there was agreement that we should, after all, have more than one eucharistic prayer. It appeared as Prayer 3 in ASB and, although manifestly popular, there were points at which editing came to be seen as desirable. For example, 'he lived on earth and went about among us' gives a stronger accent to the incarnation than 'was seen on earth and went about among us'. Inspired by the text in Hippolytus, its vivid language gives a sense of the Eucharist being a recalling of the whole of the life of Christ, and the place of the community within redemption. Hippolytus, it must be remembered, provides a eucharistic prayer in which there is no Sanctus and in which there is but one epiclesis, of a general kind – 'send your Holy Spirit upon the offering of your holy Church'.[4] Like the Second Eucharistic Prayer in the Roman Missal, there is a neat formulation after the Sanctus to lead into the first epiclesis, which would have been unknown to Hippolytus: in Prayer B it combines reference back to the Sanctus with the institution narrative to come – 'Lord, you are holy indeed, the source of all holiness; grant that by the power of your Holy Spirit and according to your holy will'. As with Prayer A the anamnesis is necessarily lengthy, but the version here is an improvement on the 1980 original, particularly because 'we bring before you this bread and this cup' no longer hangs around at the end but is an integral part of the process of memorial and offering 'our' sacrifice of praise and thanksgiving. The prayer for the Spirit on the communicants moves characteristically towards the

heavenly banquet. Perhaps scope could have been given for
short intercessions here, as with Prayers F and G. One of
the criticisms of contemporary eucharistic practice is that,
communal as it now is, it sometimes gives the impression of
being exclusively about those who receive communion
rather than everyone else – the world included, the orbit of
eucharistic mission.

Prayer C

Like B, this prayer dates back to the pre-1980 debates
before the production of the ASB, when many expressed a
desire to include elements of the Prayer Book service in the
forthcoming service book. Rather like the Roman Catholic
Church retaining the historic 'Roman Canon' as its First
Eucharistic Prayer and adding three fresh compositions, the
Church of England made a strong signal of continuity here
as the newer prayers were being composed. The 1662
Prayer Book does not have a single eucharistic prayer,
which means that this particular compilation is distanced
from it not only in the 'you-language' but in its structure as
well. But the resulting text is a success. Proper prefaces are
allowed, although not the Extended Prefaces permitted
with A, B and E because that would be unharmonious – and
repetitious – in the face of the Prayer Book imagery and
themes later on in the prayer. The paragraph following the
Sanctus begins 'All glory be to you . . .', using the same
motif as the 1764 Scottish Liturgy. Some of the editing for
the CW version reintroduces more of the Prayer Book
language – '*who* made there . . .' The anamnesis is unique:
'in remembrance . . . we offer you through him this our
sacrifice of praise and thanksgiving'. The Prayer Book rite
is never one to underplay the benefits of communion, and
this holds true when it prays that 'we and all your Church

may receive forgiveness of our sins'. This is an image which several Anglican writers of the seventeenth century interpreted as referring to considerably more than the communicants, for in the Eucharist we pray for the whole world and in the communion of saints.

Prayer D

We now come to the first of the new compositions in CW and it occupies this place because there has been a long debate about what kind of prayer is appropriate when many children are present. Despite resistance to this sort of move at all, a number of responsorial eucharistic prayers in a less conventional style of language were included in *Patterns for Worship* in 1989.[5] Prayer D, however, owes no parentage to those texts, having been composed in the context of the repeatedly expressed desire for such a prayer on the floor of General Synod and elsewhere. As Colin Buchanan and Charles Read remark, 'There is a strong emphasis on the love of God reaching out to the errant sinner.'[6] The qualification '*good* Father' obliquely refers to the fact that for many people fatherhood is not necessarily a pleasant experience – if an experience at all; and the same image is repeated at the start of the post-Sanctus – 'Father of all'. There is a strong narrative element of salvation history moving inexorably to the cross, emphasized by the short space of its linguistic compass. But it remains to be seen whether the repeated variation on the chorus of Frances Alstyne's hymn, 'Blessed assurance' – 'This is my story, this is my song' – will wear well. Brevity also means that complex ideas such as eucharistic consecration have to be expressed elliptically ('Send your Spirit on us now that by these gifts we may feed on Christ), but that in itself is no bad thing.

Prayer E

Like D, this prayer has been written partly to meet the criticism of the length of the eucharistic prayers in the ASB. However, because of the brevity of its ordinary preface, it is more likely to be used in conjunction with one or other of the Extended Prefaces; this will have the advantage of bringing to the congregation the riches of the liturgical year. The rich image of 'broken bread and wine outpoured' recalls the enthusiasm for receiving in *both* kinds in the century after the Reformation, which led, for example in many Reformed rites, to making almost as much of pouring from the flagon into the cup as breaking the bread. The anamnesis uses the expression 'plead with confidence', also to be found in Prayer G – 'plead' being a word used of the eucharistic memorial in writers going back to the seventeenth century. The shortness of the sentences in this prayer is its greatest asset, partly because the expressions are so pithy. As Buchanan and Read comment, 'its unchanging latter half gives a glimpsed vision of God's kingdom of justice and mercy'.[7] Yet if there is a gap, it is that there is no *explicit* reference to sacramental grace in the eucharistic feeding. Like Prayer B, it ends by directing the worshippers towards the heavenly feast.

Prayer F

This is another new composition but with a difference. When the three additional eucharistic prayers for the Roman Missal were compiled after the Second Vatican Council, there was a desire to use as a model a text which could lay claim to being prayed in one form or another in many of the Eastern churches. Accordingly, for the Fourth Eucharistic Prayer the version of the eucharistic prayer attributed to Basil of Caesarea and in use in the Coptic

Church was studied carefully. This was because most scholars agreed that it went back to the time of Basil himself and it was probably the source of other prayers in use in the Byzantine, Syrian and Armenian churches – an impressive array indeed. The prayer in question was rich in texture, it had a clear trinitarian shape, the Holy Spirit was (not surprisingly) given full mention, and all was set within a strong narrative of salvation history. Another version was produced for ecumenical use in North America that was more faithful to the shape of the original (Roman 4 introduces the 'split' epiclesis, a singularly un-Eastern feature), which appears in the 1979 *Book of Common Prayer* of ECUSA and the 1985 *Book of Alternative Services* of the Anglican Church in Canada. There were those who thought that CW should contain a fresh composition in the style and approach of these 'Basilian' prayers, complete with some of the responses in the Eastern originals.[8] The responses in the CW text, which could be led by a deacon, are optional, although like most responses in these prayers they come over better sung rather than said. Unlike any of the prayers so far, but like Prayer G, the section coming between the dialogue and the Sanctus is about creation – 'by the breath of your mouth you have spoken your word and all things have come into being'. The language also stresses the paradox of redemption: after the Sanctus, 'Lord God, you are the most holy one, enthroned in splendour and light, yet in the coming of your Son Jesus Christ you reveal the power of your love made perfect in our human weakness.' Like A and G, the anamnesis is strong on verbs: 'proclaim', 'celebrate', 'rejoice', 'long for'; and like G, it continues to use powerful verbs: 'form', 'make', 'look', 'gather'. It is perhaps a pity that the epiclesis is not as bold as was originally proposed, a mark of unfinished business. But its trinitarian focus – there is no need of proper prefaces of any kind with such a prayer – marks it off as a significant addition and (one hopes) a long-term ecumenical investment.

Prayer G

This prayer has its origins in a text compiled by the Roman Catholic International Commission on English in the Liturgy in 1984 entitled 'An Original Eucharistic Prayer'.[9] Because of the rich and innovative character of some of its imagery, it formed the basis of one of the prayers included in *Patterns for Worship* in 1989.[10] However, some changes were made; the prayer was shortened and modelled along Eastern lines, with a single epiclesis; and scope was provided for seasonal insertions. It also used the verb 'plead' for the first time in an Anglican liturgy,[11] although it had been used by a number of writers, Anglican, Reformed, and Roman Catholic, which may be one of reasons why the 1989 version attracted ecumenical interest. There are some special features. 'Silent music' comes directly from John of the Cross's *Spiritual Canticle*.[12] 'The crown of all creation' is a commonplace patristic theme, placing human nature at the apex of God's creation but intrinsically part of it. 'As a mother tenderly gathers her children' brings in an important feminine biblical image (Isa. 66.13; Matt. 23.37). The verbs in the later part are full of images of creation and redemption: 'form', 'build', 'bring' (cf. Eph. 2.20–21; 4.13–16). And the concluding reference to 'the vision of that eternal splendour for which you have created us' is inspired by Kenneth Kirk's great book, *The Vision of God*.[13] Like Prayer F there are intercessions, though here they are optional, which makes both prayers suitable for occasions when another sacrament or rite has taken place at the end of the Liturgy of the Word. It is a pity that, as in

Prayer E, 'with confidence' was added after 'we plead' and that the epiclesis was flattened. In the interests of simplicity, the seasonal insertions in the 1989 text were not included (they are perhaps ripe for reappearance). The imagery of this prayer is tightly packed, partly because it emerged at a stage when there was a desire to develop pictorial language.

Prayer H

This prayer was written in the last stages of the revision process leading up to the publication of CW, but a prayer written and revised under pressure is not necessarily lacking in quality. There was a strong signal from those who were critical of the traditional-style eucharistic prayer that there should be a fully 'interactive' text along the lines of some local experiments. Unique among these prayers, this text ends with the Sanctus, a factor which makes conclusion a bit of a problem although this can be met by introducing the Lord's Prayer in words which resonate with 'kingdom'. The near opening line, 'in your love you made us for yourself' is inspired by the famous words near the start of Augustine's *Confessions* ('you made us for yourself and our hearts are restless until they find their rest in you'), and 'welcomed us to sit and eat with you' by George Herbert's 'Love bade me welcome'.[14] In such a short compass the prayer manages to says what needs to be said – just – and the unitive 'we offer you this sacrifice of praise' at the end draws its themes together. But it would be a pity if, just because of its brevity and interactive nature, it became the only prayer used among some congregations.

Extended Prefaces

There are no fewer than eighteen of these and they take
their inspiration from the new Roman Missal. Some of
them are adapted from the Roman originals, others are
taken from the new version of the Sacramentary, others
again are fresh compositions. Like the eucharistic prayers
in general, they repay careful attention. The text for use in
what is sometimes called 'Ordinary Time' has the resurrection for its theme, with the resonant reference to living 'in
endless light'. The two Advent texts fit the two aspects of
the season, the first stressing the divine plan, the second the
coming of John the Baptist. Christmas celebrates the God
who is made visible to us in Christ. The Epiphany preface
tells of the three wonders – the Magi, the Baptism of Christ
and the marriage at Cana. Candlemas gives us a rich
portrait of the festival, with Anna present as well as
Simeon, and the sword that will pierce the Virgin's soul.
Ash Wednesday draws out the three Lenten themes of fast-
ing, penitence and catechesis. The Annunciation preface
captures the way in which this feast always (and rightly)
gets in the way of the Easter cycle – 'from the warmth of her
womb to the stillness of the grave'. The later Lenten text
takes us to the cross: 'the whole world is called to acknowl-
edge his hidden majesty'. For Maundy Thursday, the foot-
washing drama is central in the Upper Room of the Last
Supper. Easter Day celebrates humanity placed once more
in paradise. Ascension Day is perhaps too exclusively
paschal and not strong enough on the Day itself. After
Ascension we celebrate Christ who has gone before us, and
at Pentecost the giving of the Spirit to proclaim the gospel.
Both the Trinity and All Saints' texts cleverly use material
from the Te Deum ('Father of majesty unbounded' and
'The glorious company of apostles praise you'). For the

pre-Advent Sundays, Christ is seen as the hope of the nations; and for Christ the King, the Saviour is hailed as the anointed one. Finally, the Saints' Day formula sets our celebration in the heavenly call of the saints, who surround us in our pilgrimage. It is a rich collection, perhaps lacking provision for martyrs, a small omission.[15]

15 COMMUNION

The Lord's Prayer

As the Eucharist turns towards the act of communion, there are various devices used to mark this significant moment. From the early accounts, there is not much to tell – perhaps no more than a functional switch. But there has long been some kind of transitional section, the better for the People of God to prepare themselves for the moment in the service which marks it off as unique: receiving the consecrated bread and wine.

The first transition takes the form of the Lord's Prayer.[1] Without doubt the most used and interpreted of all Christian prayers, it was probably inevitable that it should find a place in the Eucharist. Although it has long been a kind of measuring-stick for intercession, especially personal intercession, its position in the Eucharist has from early times been here – before the communion. Early teaching about the Lord's Prayer derives from baptismal preparation, resulting in the candidates having to recite it aloud, along with the Creed, at their baptism. How Christians were to pray and what they were supposed to believe thus took on a public priority and as infant baptism increasingly became the norm, so godparents took on the role of teaching the growing child these two emblems of Christianity.

Faced with its central place in baptismal preparation and

at the baptismal liturgy, the Church had to find a corres-
pondingly central place for this prayer in the Eucharist and
it is easy to see why reciting it before receiving communion
was the solution. It is not just a case of the 'daily bread'
being referred to the Eucharist, but the other themes as
well, not least forgiveness for the past and protection in the
future. Augustine, preaching in the early fifth century in
North Africa, saw the link between baptism and eucharist
when he used to say that by asking to be forgiven daily at
the altar we are in fact recalling our baptism, when that
forgiveness was imparted to us at the font.

But there is another unique feature to this prayer at the
Eucharist and it concerns how it is introduced. Not all the
old liturgies prescribe it to be said by *all*. The old Spanish
rite directs the priest to say each petition on his own, the
congregation replying with an Amen each time. But it was
usually the only prayer said by all. It was also important
that everyone should join in with the resounding opening
words – 'Our Father'. The claim – that God is our 'Abba',
an intimate yet respected father – is echoed on two occasions by Paul in his epistles, which could possibly be some
kind of coded reference to the prayer itself, even though
Paul does not give us the full text (Rom. 8.14–16; Gal. 4.6).
Such considerations as these gave rise to the view that the
prayer needed to be introduced. Overall, there were two
themes used, the Fatherhood of God and our daring to be
able to address him in prayer, and our state of being a
forgiven people. The first was used in the Roman rite, and
the second is what we find in several of the Eastern rites. 'As
our Saviour taught us, so we pray' is thus a somewhat limp
version of the older form, translating the Roman version,
'As our Saviour hath commanded and taught us, we *are
bold* to say'. There is no (at least official) scope in CW for
varying the introduction to this prayer, probably because

the two introductions are intended to signal which version is to be used.

This brings us to consider the question of the version of the prayer. The fact of the matter is that this beloved prayer has been translated into languages (and dialects) for many centuries as an essential vehicle of mission and prayer. There have been different vernacular versions used in this country for over a thousand years. And, moreover, even in the face of the various texts in use in the late Middle Ages, it took some time before a 'definitive' text was issued with the First Prayer Book of 1549.[2] The reason why we have two in use today is that we have not yet made up our mind which it is to be! The first text is the internationally agreed version, except that the Church of England has doggedly adhered to the more ambiguous 'lead us not into temptation' rather than the more specific 'do not bring us to the time of trial', although *that* version is included in CW in the 'Prayers for Various Occasions', with a hint for its suitability for ecumenical use. The second is the updated traditional version which has been in use for over thirty years, with 'who art', 'on earth', and 'those who trespass', instead of 'which art', 'in earth', and 'them that trespass'. This variety is a source of concern to many but it is a sign of a time of transition. In any case, to have different versions may have the disadvantage of a lack of unanimity but it has the advantage of alerting people to what they are actually saying, particularly in the case of a prayer that can trip off the tongue too easily.

How should the prayer end? The earliest manuscripts of the Lord's Prayer in the New Testament (Matt. 6.9–13 and Luke 11.2–4) contain no doxology, 'for the kingdom, the power, and the glory are yours, now and for ever'. But the need to conclude with such an ascription of praise, following the pattern of Jewish prayer, seemed irresistible, and in the early Christian manual, the *Didache*, we find the Lord's Prayer with this doxology but without the 'kingdom'.[3] Once again, there is a difference of practice. In the East, the doxology is always included at the Eucharist, in line with their love of ascriptions of praise at the end of prayer. But the doxology was never part of the Roman rite at all – that is, until after the Second Vatican Council, when it comes (in the Eucharist only) after the short prayer 'Deliver us, Lord, from every evil . . .' which has followed the main text of the Lord's Prayer for many centuries. At the Reformation, the doxology was included in several of the versions of the Bible, which is why it came to be used with the Lord's Prayer in public worship. Although the Prayer Book sometimes has the doxology and sometimes leaves it out, the practice nowadays is always to include it.

All these matters – of how to introduce the prayer, how to translate it, and how to conclude it – are going to vary from one tradition to another. There will be new translations of the Lord's Prayer in the centuries to come. But much more importantly, Christians will always want to recite or sing this prayer as they approach the Lord's Table.

Breaking of the bread

The breaking of a loaf of bread is an action which is required whenever bread is to be eaten and, like the placing of the bread and cup on the holy table before the great eucharistic prayer, it is a functional act which has symbolic overtones that are inescapable. Paul sees this clearly when in writing to the Corinthians he observes: 'Because there is one bread, we who are many are one body, for we all partake of the one bread' (1 Cor. 10.17). And many liturgies ancient and modern have used this verse, either directly or indirectly, in this context.

But how are the actions to be matched to the words? As with the offertory, there can be problems, because not everything that should be seen can be seen. I recall a cathedral canon who used to raise a large piece of wafer bread and break it in two above his head and then bring the two pieces down onto the paten in what looked like a single sweeping motion. It certainly brought home to a large congregation what was happening and almost made the words superfluous. It is not always possible to 'break' the bread dramatically but care needs to be given as to how it is done and the most appropriate ways of doing so. After all, this particular section begins with a direction – like the preparation of the altar earlier – and not with words. Drama can be overdone but it can also be underdone. In a small side-chapel it is almost pointless to break the bread in such a covert, minimalistic way that no one can see. The breaking of the bread is the main feature of this, the second preparatory part of the service before communion.

There are other forms of words to be used at this point. The alternative response, 'every time we eat this bread . . .' is also taken from Paul writing to the Corinthians, this time from the end of his narrative of the institution of the supper (1 Cor. 11.26). And then come two versions of the ancient hymn, the Agnus Dei. This was probably first used in Syria and inspired by John the Baptist's address to Jesus near the start of the Fourth Gospel (John 1.29, 36). It was introduced at Rome towards the end of the seventh century by Pope Sergius I (687–701), in order to cover the time taken to prepare the bread for distribution of communion, and the same line was repeated until all was ready. The last line was changed to 'grant us peace' to form a conclusion and also to link with the giving of the Peace, which in the Roman rite takes place soon after. The second version of the 'Agnus Dei' was composed by Geoffrey Cuming some years ago and is a free rendition, in which the plural of the Latin 'peccata' is definitely translated as 'sins'; the Latin plural was intended to translate the Greek singular, which is supposed to express the great expanse of God's love. The 'sin' of the world also echoes the same expression in the Gloria in excelsis and the invitation to communion.

It is worth pausing for a moment to look at the images and use of these formulae, which come from such different eras and places, whether it is the Pauline epistles or a Syrian pope adapting a hymn familiar to him to cover an elaborate action at a grand-scale papal mass. The Pauline formulae stress the action of the Eucharist, and they have an immediacy that is direct and appealing. The Agnus Dei, however, regardless of the version, takes us into a different milieu, that of devotional prayer to Jesus himself. That change of focus should not be ignored, for a prayer to Jesus as the Lamb of God has a more intimate character, the Lamb of sacrifice who gives life to the world – life which is about mercy and peace. This might suggest that the Pauline formulae and the Agnus Dei should be alternatives, instead of the requirement that the former must be said and the Agnus Dei is optional. On the other hand, there are occasions when the Agnus Dei is sung to elaborate choral settings, in which case it comes more appropriately during communion, otherwise the service will be held up. Yet again, the Pauline formulae may suit a house-group celebration better on its own.

Finally there is the additional image of pouring, which occurs frequently in the post-Reformation writers and preachers for the understandable reason that they were enthused by the reintroduction of giving the cup to the laity. Among them, Lancelot Andrewes frequently refers to the eucharistic elements as 'conduit-pipes' of God's grace, in a clear echo of the sacramental cup.[4] Richard Baxter

(1615–91) followed Puritan practice in making as much of the breaking of the bread as of the pouring of the wine from the flagon into the cup. The words used at this point are interestingly reminiscent of the Agnus Dei: 'We were redeemed with the precious blood of Christ, as of a Lamb without blemish and without spot.'[5]

This preparatory part of the Eucharist can usefully become what it is meant to be, the preparation of the elements for the distribution. There is a lot to be said for having only one chalice and a flagon on the altar up to this point and for the remaining chalices to be brought forward later and consecrated wine poured into them from the flagon. It would certainly save fuss at the preparation of the table. The breaking of the bread and the pouring of the wine are actions that need to be carried out but the People of God need to be devotionally fed at the same time, hence the time-honoured singing of the Agnus Dei.

Giving of communion

The Lord's Prayer has been said and the bread and wine are now ready for the distribution of communion. It remains to bid the People of God to share in the Lord's Supper. And as with the breaking of the bread, there are two sets of material – invitation, which is mandatory, and devotion, which is optional.

The invitation to communion is self-explanatory and the different forms used throughout history have varied in their details. The four in CW come from different sources. The first is an amalgam of the invitation to confession and the words of distribution in the Prayer Book, 'Draw near'. The second is an adaptation of the corresponding formula in the Roman mass, substituting 'Jesus' for 'This' in order not to overlocalize the eucharistic presence, and 'blessed' for 'happy' in order to sound more trenchant; it echoes images in the New Testament (John 1.29; Rev. 19.9; and Matt. 8.8). The third is an adaptation of the form used throughout the East since the fourth century – 'holy things for holy persons'. And the fourth, 'Christ our Passover', is similar to what was used at this point in the 1549 Prayer Book, and once again is based on Pauline material (1 Cor. 5. 7–8).

This is quite an assembly of sources – Prayer Book, Roman-biblical, Eastern and Pauline. And each is different in tone. The first invites and exhorts. The second states, with a devotional response. The third – as does the fourth, in a different way – states and invites in the same register. How should one choose? The fourth is suggested for the Easter season, which is self-evident, though it is equally appropriate on other occasions. It would be a pity if different groups in the church went exclusively for one of the others, with lovers of the Prayer Book opting for the first, Anglo-Catholics opting for the second, and enthusiasts of the Greek Fathers opting for the third. Not one of them teaches anything significantly different from another.

Finally, we come to what has since the seventeenth century been called the Prayer of Humble Access.[6] The first (and older) form has an interesting history. It appeared in the 1549 Prayer Book immediately before communion, moving to a slightly earlier position in 1552 and remaining there in 1662. In 1971 it was placed much earlier, just before the Peace, and made optional, with an additional version of the prayer in the same genre, which is what we find in the ASB. In CW it is restored to its original position but is optional.

A classic of devotional literature, it breathes a rich atmosphere of eucharistic piety which it is important not to lose. In the later Middle Ages there was a strong tradition of devotional prayers throughout the mass, inspired by the oft-used formula, 'Lord, I am not worthy' (Matt. 8.8), which began to appear in local rites from the tenth century onwards. Only a century later, the great Benedictine theologian and Archbishop of Canterbury, Anselm (c. 1033–1109) composed a pre-communion devotional prayer, probably for his own use when celebrating mass, which begins in the same way and it is more than likely that Cranmer had it open in front of him when compiling 'We do not presume', weaving other biblical echoes into it.[7] At any rate, many liturgies contain some kind of corresponding prayer and it is good that we have a text like this in the Anglican repertoire which arises out of the creative use of medieval forms at the Reformation. The alternative version uses images from George Herbert, as well as many biblical echoes (e.g. Matt. 22.1–10 and 15.27). But as with the Agnus Dei in relation to the words at the breaking of the bread, so here it must be asked: Are the words of invitation really necessary when the Prayer of Humble Access is to be said? It is clear from the words of the prayer that the communicants intend to communicate, for neither prayer suggests a withdrawal, but rather a God-given confidence in the Saviour's mercy. As Baldwin of Ford, a Cistercian monk who eventually became Archbishop of Canterbury in 1184, once wrote: 'In taking our nature, Christ in the same way took the bread. Christ took the means to nourish us, because he was united to humanity by the mystery of the Incarnation.'[8] For now, it is time for words to cease and for the sacramental feeding to happen – in God's own good time and space.

16 CONCLUSION

After communion

> At your mystical supper, Son of God,
> receive me today as a partaker,
> for I will not betray the sacrament to your enemies,
> nor give you a kiss like Judas,
> but like the thief I confess you:
> remember me, Lord, in your Kingdom.[1]

These are the words which are sung during the distribution of communion in the Orthodox Liturgy on Maundy Thursday and it is not hard to see why they are so appropriate. Judas's betrayal of Jesus, planned before the Last Supper and effected after it, forms a backdrop to Maundy Thursday. But there is a sense in which this early sixth-century chant, unusual for its non-scriptural base, comes to every eucharist. How faithful are we? How effective as instruments of reconciliation are we going to be, not only in the tangled web of our own personal contradictions but in our localities and the wider world? For the moment of receiving communion points back to the last time we received and forward to the next time we come to the table. Not only that, but as the very word implies, communion is an act of sharing, which means kneeling or standing alongside or near others who might have callings and tasks and

attitudes in this life of which we strongly disapprove. Why
not gather instead for a good, long session of indoctrina-
tion? Because we have not gathered to celebrate correct
ideas vigorously but to follow a person more faithfully, and
that makes our sharing costly in every sense. Like Judas,
we are in all likelihood going to betray Christ, whether
willingly or not, as well as betray the sacrament to the
Lord's enemies – in other words, not to take its overwhelming demands to heart. And we will come once more
to the table for forgiveness and feeding.

What I have received is indeed 'beyond words' (2 Cor.
9.15) and I know that I will spend a great deal of my life
coming to terms with it. In a recent book, David Ford looks
at this phenomenon which he calls 'the eucharistic self'.[2]
Many are the influences that form it and at this point in the
liturgy, it is worth pondering the different words of distribution. They may be the Prayer Book form, stating what is
given and then beckoning us to eat and drink faithfully. Or
they may be one of the other, briefer forms, stating directly
('the body of Christ'), or more elusively, along the lines
of the *Apostolic Tradition* of Hippolytus ('The bread of
heaven in Christ Jesus'). The 'eucharistic self' is the faithful
Christian coping with receiving God's free gift in community and as individual. The self is surrounded by a 'habitus',
a tradition, a building, liturgical colour and clothing. In a
rich texture of ritual actions, at the heart of which are the
simple commands to 'take' and 'drink' and 'do this', the act
of communion is *the* moment of incorporation into a new
community, a new understanding of selfhood.

The Eucharist's radical *difference* from the world, so far
from being the tamed repetition of false identity, a sense of
belonging to an irrelevant past, is in reality a way of seeing
a fragmented world yearning for what it was always meant
to be – made new and whole. Ford goes on to expound the

eucharistic self, what we may call here in more traditional terms the communicant, as 'blessed' by an all-embracing God; 'placed' once more face to face with Christ; 'timed' in a new world, yet still within the distractions (and there will be many) of family, work, television; and 'commanded' to live more faithfully, which is not to be seen as the prerequisite for us being there, but rather the purpose for which we are sent out.[3] This is why 'Communion' is a sacrifice, a meal shared in the presence of God, as a means of grace, and a suggestion of discipleship's cost. Dietrich Bonhoeffer describes the eucharistic journey as follows:

> The day of the Lord's Supper is an occasion of joy for the Christian community. Reconciled in their hearts with God and the brethren, the congregation receives the gift of the body and blood of Jesus Christ, and receiving that, it receives forgiveness, new life, and salvation. It is given new fellowship with God and men. The fellowship of the Lord's Supper is the superlative fulfilment of Christian fellowship. As the members of the congregation are united in body and blood at the table of the Lord so will they be together in eternity. Here the community has reached its goal. Here joy in Christ and his community is complete. The life of Christians together under the Word has reached its perfection in the sacrament.[4]

Now is the time to use the space by focusing on one particular thing and not several. It may be a helpful idea in the sermon, or a thought in the intercessions, or even back in the confession, when I said, 'Forgive what we have been, help us to amend what we are, and direct what we shall be'. Now is the time to be specific in what we are dwelling upon. There will be times when this will be easier than others, and God is capable of using distractions even if we

are bothered by them ourselves. But the effort of concentration repays. In times past, there was more stillness at
communion. From that devotional world, Teresa of Avila,
a sixteenth-century nun, wrote an extended meditation on
the Lord's Prayer as part of her desire to reform her Spanish
Carmelite nuns: 'Delight to remain with Him; do not lose
such an excellent time for talking with Him as the hour
after Communion.'[5] We may not have an hour to spare but
we can still converse with Christ, listening perhaps rather
than speaking first. The empty space may provide a vital
clue to our lives. We may be able to recognize it all the
better if we observe its space and heed its calling to enjoy
Holy Communion, and that means thinking about our
fellow-communicants as well as those who are present but
for one reason or another not able to partake. We are one
with them, whether we like them or not.

Prayer after communion

The silence after communion is sometimes most effective
when there has been a lot of noise, and that means everyone
being still, from musicians to churchwardens. The individual's response to this silence will vary, as has just been
suggested. But the collective silence is another kind of
statement, more than the mere fact that one particular communicant is waiting – however creatively! – for the final
part of the service to begin. The congregation's silence is a
chance for the entire gathering to refocus itself, to become
aware again of its character as a community rather than a
collection of individuals who happen to be at the same
event. Sometimes the silence will be a powerful sense of
purpose – a national tragedy offered to God, the newly
married who have just made their vows, or a communion
hymn that has said exactly what needed to be said and the

musicians have entered into its spirit in just the right way. Of course there will be occasions when the silence is fidgety and distracting, but those troughs are worth going through in order to experience the heights as well. Above all, congregations need to know roughly how long the silence is going to be, unless it is a house-group celebration and the sense of unity is strong enough already. It is perhaps worth noting that the silence forms part of the Prayer after Communion, and is not a mere preamble to it.

The spoken prayers which follow come in two forms, the first of which is optional and said by the president, and the second mandatory and said by all. The optional prayers are those which vary according to the season. Their restoration to the Anglican Eucharist is welcome, because they go back in the West to the early centuries. A variable post-communion prayer provides the opportunity to bring seasonal (or occasional) concerns into the open. For example, the Ascension Day prayer appropriately asks that 'we may set our hearts in the heavenly places', and that suggested for use at baptism prays, 'preserve in your people the new life of baptism'. As with the Collects, many different sources, ancient and modern, have gone into their production and their quality will be seen over the years as people come to know them better and pray them with familiarity.[6] The basic shape of these prayers is to give thanks for receiving the sacrament and to ask for the graces of the time or occasion to live more faithfully.

The second prayer is mandatory and said by all. There is a choice from the two which appeared in ASB. One is a brief thanksgiving, leading into a short act of self-offering. (It is a pity that no effort was made to draw more of the theme of self-offering from the Prayer Book original.) The other is a longer, more devotional composition, also written for ASB. It paints a picture of the prodigal son being

received back and then, like the apostles, illumined by
Christ, after which we are anchored in the hope of Christ.
It is a rich prayer, which some local service booklets suggest
for personal rather public use during the distribution of
communion.

The Dismissal

We have now reached the final section of the service which,
like the Gathering, has implications of architecture and the
use of space. On the surface, it is straightforward, because
it is about blessing and dismissing. But where should it
come and when? The hymn comes now, so that the congregation's thanksgiving is gathered together in song, having
been spoken in verbal prayer which in turn draws together
the thoughts of silent prayer. And the Dismissal should be
said *before* any procession moves off, for the Dismissal is
about everyone, not just those in the nave as they wait for
the procession to leave. I recall once going to mass in a
French town and being struck by how appropriate it was
for everyone to leave the moment the dismissal had been
given. It was no announcement but a command. There is
nothing more to be said, nothing to wait for. In many
places, the Notices are given out just before the blessing, so
that they do not get in the way of anything else – far better
here than right at the start, or – even worse – between the
Gospel and the sermon. Often overdone ('You will find all
the notices printed on the leaflet, but I just want to draw
your attention to each one of them in turn . . .'), they are an
essential part of parish communication and like everything
else need careful preparation.

   The Dismissal, therefore, performs exactly the function
its title implies. Things have come to an end. The notion of
giving a blessing crept into the early medieval mass to serve

as a kind of compensation for those who were not going to receive communion – an increasing proportion of the congregation. At first given only by the bishop, the blessing came to be given also by priests with the result that it became a feature of every eucharist, never having belonged there in the first place. But the blessing has come to be regarded as essential, in spite of attempts to make it optional. The theorists maintain that the greatest form of blessing is to receive the sacrament, while the pragmatists will insist that people expect and want it and it is impossible to turn the clock back to an ancient form of eucharist that may never have been celebrated. The form of blessing suggested for ordinary occasions in CW is the same as that which appeared in the 1549 Prayer Book – 'The peace of God . . .' (Phil. 4.7). The many other forms suggested for other seasons and occasions are often similarly inspired by the Bible, for example that for Easter: 'The God of peace, who brought again from the dead our Lord Jesus, that great shepherd of the sheep . . .' (Heb. 13.20). And the fact that we are called 'the Easter people' makes it appropriate to sing 'Alleluia!' in the dismissal in the Easter season.

'The ministers and people depart' is how the service ends. Nothing could be more fitting than these simple words, and nothing more rich and complex in their implications for each person present. Which is why the Eucharist is designed to bring everyone back – for more. This truth is expressed in a poem entitled 'After Communion' by the nineteenth-century poet, Christina Rossetti. She reflects on the images of Christ's kingship, and how he bridges the gap between our lives and the life of heaven:

Why should I call Thee Lord, Who art my God?
Why should I call Thee Friend, Who art my Love?
Or King, Who art my very Spouse above?

Or call Thy Sceptre on my heart Thy rod?
Lo, now Thy banner over me is love
All heaven flies open to me at Thy nod:
For Thou hast lit Thy flame in me a clod,
Made me a nest for dwelling of Thy Dove.
What wilt Thou call me in our home above,
Who now hast called me friend? How will it be
When Thou for good wine settest forth the best?
Now Thou dost bid me come and sup with Thee,
Now Thou dost make me lean upon Thy breast:
How will it be with me in time of love?[7]

EPILOGUE: WHAT OF THE FUTURE?

What we have

> The risk of postmodernism is that of enclosure in text, without reference to the unenclosed truth or to the ineffable of the subject, as it were both beneath and beyond language.[1]

So wrote the American Roman Catholic scholar, David N. Power, at the end of a groundbreaking ecumenical study of the Eucharist, in which he looks quizzically at the past and present and attempts to look into the future. There is much worth pondering in what he says. This is especially true of formulating liturgical texts that are both resonant and faithful to the ongoing quest for doctrinal consensus, as well as faithful to the changing needs of the Church. Power's implied judgement – that we need to trust those words, actions and contexts rather more than we sometimes do – does not mean that we must stop thinking critically. But it leaves us with a sense of the provisional – and that is no bad thing, however much toil, thought and effort went into the production of the current service-book, regardless of the church in question.

As one looks into the future, a number of questions surface as unfinished business. The first is the plethora of variables. A noble provision in themselves – the flow and

content of Prayer F is a case in point – there nonetheless
remains the issue of how the Church at large is going to
cope with them without destabilizing its collective memory.
The overall shape of the liturgy may be clearer and the
irreducible minimum of the service sharper than in preceding years, but the sheer amount of variables gives the
impression that the words themselves may not be entirely
trustworthy or at least as authoritative as they might be.
This is arguably the case in relation to the Creeds and the
Affirmations of Faith, where the revisers might have been
wiser to have adopted a more restrictive path. There is a
great difference between the historic Creeds of the Church
and Affirmations of Faith that may be used on certain occasions, yet one doubts if this distinction is going to continue
to be as clear as it should be. The end result may well be
that much of this material is not going to be used; in the
clamour for alternatives, the revisers were doing what they
were bidden but the next stage – as with some modern
hymn-books – is likely to be a process of pruning.

   Secondly, there is the question of how the assembly
gathers. This is – rightly – identified as a liturgically significant focus. But it means much more than the physical and
spiritual actions of preparation and meeting. What we are
experiencing in today's Church is a profound sense of frag-
mentation, in which it is becoming increasingly difficult to
locate the 'Christian community' in one particular occasion.
The three prototypes identified earlier – the house communion, the big assembly, the side-altar – are probably
going to become increasingly important in the future, with
the big assembly relying more and more on the other two,
in style as well as ethos. To 'gather' appropriately in those
very different contexts will require careful observation and
thought; the big occasion will stand out more and more,
where a group of local congregations in a rural area, for

example, meet together as part of their own sense of 'communion' (local rivalries notwithstanding!), when for the rest of the time they may need to learn to use their buildings in a different way that is more appropriate for a smaller congregation. The home-based celebration – for which compositions like Prayer H, for all its faults, could be a winner – will probably continue to develop, whether for the house-bound, the house-group, or people at work. But in those provisional arenas, it needs to be realized that small congregations are part of something much larger. Too much local 'tailoring' can undermine local catholicity, for one of the formative characteristics of the community is its sense of being part of a common narrative.[2]

Thirdly, there is the question of forgiveness as a process. The penitential flavour of parts of the Prayer Book has left a legacy behind that is not easily shaken off, yet the paschal and celebratory tone of many a contemporary eucharist asks implicit questions about exactly what kind of place forgiveness should have at all – over and above the very truth that the Lord's Supper is a celebration of the new life given us by the cross. By placing the confession near the start, the revisers fell into line with other modern texts and there is much to be said in an ecumenical age for going with that flow. But there is a deeper issue at stake here and it concerns how forgiveness is to be held onto as a uniquely Christian truth and experience, over against a popular view which goes no further than regret; Rowan Williams has recently drawn attention to our inability as a society to cope with remorse and shame.[3] The purely *verbal* character of the opening confession, rich though the language can be and heartfelt though it may be uttered, nonetheless may cry out on occasion for the use of symbolism – baptismal water, ashing – as an enactment, a disclosure, of the mystery of our unearned forgiveness by the Loving God.

Such public symbols of forgiveness may go hand in hand with the way in which the Church is often at the forefront of local – and national – issues of reconciliation. The relationship between baptism (celebrated once for each) and eucharist (celebrated frequently for all) is ripe for further development, for there is an inherently *baptismal* aspect of forgiveness, a constant redirecting of heart and mind towards the Living God.

Fourthly, there is the question of eucharistic theology. We are fortunate to have had the advantage of using ecumenical agreements and a wealth of eucharistic theology, not least the rich tradition of Anglican writing. The two historic no-go areas of presence and sacrifice have been loosened up considerably. We now know – and can increasingly digest – that in the early centuries these concepts were freer from precise definition than was once thought to be the case, whether by conservative Roman Catholics or traditionalist Protestants. The bread and wine become really and spiritually the Body and Blood of Christ, in a manner that defies scientific definition, and they are signs of the sacrifice of Christ, because bread and wine are themselves the result of dying and rising. Christ is present – to use Calvin's language, 'in virtue and in power'[4] – both at the table and on the table, as he offers himself to us in bread and wine. As many of the Anglican divines insisted, the Eucharist is above all the action of Christ in his Church. Much of this is expressed in the new eucharistic prayers. But they could have gone further. A wider reading of the Eastern Fathers (as was the case with the seventeenth-century Anglican divines) has indeed enabled us to understand more fully the centrality of the work of the Spirit at the Eucharist. Yet those who continue to reject the explicit blessing of inanimate objects on scriptural grounds (and who therefore oppose the explicit invoking of the Holy

Spirit on the elements of bread and wine) need to look afresh at the New Testament, where oil (James 5.14), clay (John 9.11) and spittle (Mark 7.33, 8.23) are all used as vehicles of spiritual blessing, to say nothing of the woman touching the hem of Jesus' garment (Mark 5.27ff.), and the use of handkerchiefs and aprons for healing after contact with the body of Paul (Acts 19.12). Perhaps a key text is 1 Tim. 4.4f.: 'For everything created by God is good, and nothing is to be rejected, provided it is received with thanksgiving; for it is sanctified by God's works and by prayer.'[5] Similarly, while the formulations about sacrifice are richer than before, there is still a noticeable hesitation about uniting the celebration of the Eucharist with the eternal self-offering of Christ in heaven. Again, this takes us to the New Testament, to the Last Supper narratives, for 'Jesus identified his own sacrificial death in the appearances of the action he performed at the Last Supper.'[6] This is a truth which is manifested at every eucharist by the dramatic shift from the 'we-language' of the rest of the prayer to the 'I-language' of the institution narrative. The words of Jesus then become the words of Christ in the Church.

The dynamic of tradition

There are many other pointers to the future. For example, the desire to 'flatten' the Eucharist into the confines of our own age and the particular occasion is expressed by those who want to abandon liturgical dress altogether. On the other hand, the desire for the Eucharist on every conceivable occasion can subtly undermine a sense that the Eucharist emerges out of other acts of worship, daily prayer included, and leads into the supreme outworking of worship – which is everyday life. But we are left with a provisional liturgy, and our task is so to use it, understand its many

disciplines, and above all to love it and to pray it. Our forebears were more or less content to use a fixed text for a
usually occasional communion, and they supplemented
that text with different kinds of devotional manuals, which
explored many different theological standpoints, with
prayers for preparation, thanksgiving and meditation
before, during and after the celebration. By contrast, we
have a more fluid text which can move in many different
directions, including towards private prayer and study.
Rather than being overwhelmed by the contours of those
movements, our task is to get hold of them and to be
nurtured by them. For the Eucharist's work is above all to
lead us 'beneath and beyond' the actions and the words, to
the Crucified and Living One – who will always welcome us
to eat and drink in his presence. The Eucharist will therefore *always* come back for more – regardless of how we 'do
this' at the earthly altar.

Meanwhile, we have far more than newly published
books at our disposal, for the Eucharist is about more than
an agreed and authorized text. As we have suggested
throughout this exploration of the shape, style and meaning of the contemporary Eucharist, there is a driving force
behind what we are trying to do at this altar that is fundamentally the work of God, graciously manifested in the
Scriptures, tradition, reason and experience. Together
these four givens provide the means of discovering the most
authentic way of celebrating the Holy Communion. In our
time, the way in which they have helped to provide unity,
convergence, stability and an ordered spontaneity is something of a contrast with the chaos and misery which has
known many more dying as a result of warfare and violence
in the twentieth century than in all the preceding centuries
put together – in which the Eucharist is uniquely a sign of
reconciliation in the midst of brokenness.

But the diversity – now more in style than substance – is a mark of the enduring strength of the Eucharist as it is located in the life of all the churches. Although we have concentrated on the Church of England's *Common Worship* liturgy, many of the same observations in doctrine, liturgy and presentation would, one suspects, have appeared in a comparable study of one of the other mainstream churches. And in the world-wide Anglican Communion, the diversity that was apparent, for example, at the 1998 Lambeth Conference shows remarkable signs of a common family likeness: the Philippine Eucharist may have begun with the arresting sound of a gong, signalling the entry procession, and there may have been other examples of local cultures coming through, but the liturgy was still recognizably a possession of the whole of the Church Catholic. All this indicates a common culture, confident about ways of appropriating the past and equally confident about moving into the future. But there are still challenges before us.

> Our interpretation of life always goes wrong when we focus our attention on one spot, and try to find in this the clue to all the rest. The eyes of worship have a wide-angle lens. They take in and resume a great stretch of experience, not only that which is immediately useful to man – nothing distorts reality so much as the utilitarian point of view – and in the light of this great vision they see human life, and interpret it, in a larger, nobler, more enduring way.[7]

These words come from a lecture by Evelyn Underhill at a College of Education in 1937, and they are as true today as they were then. They speak of an important dimension to the almost overwhelming opportunity of education through mission which confronts the churches now. We are indeed entrusted with a wide-angle lens, in a narrow-angle world which is tempted to look at so many things in the flat, yet shows so many signs of needing to find a means whereby we can – in common – explore the deep truths of life. Vague 'spirituality' is not up to this task, but the flesh and blood of humanity, fed by the flesh and blood of Christ can – whatever cultural forms are used. Access to the holy table is always a question with which the Church has to live. There are occasions when it is not appropriate to offer the Eucharist, but the truth of the matter is that the Eucharist, more than any other act of worship, has the innate capacity to challenge utilitarianism. It needs to be liberated to do so. That leaves us with the enduring question of continuity.

In his recent work, *Discipleship and Imagination*, David Brown makes the challenging observation that 'the real question for continuity must be what becomes appropriate under new conditions of knowledge, new forms of culture'.[8] This is a dynamic view of how the catholicity of the Church develops. There has certainly been a high degree of 'new conditions of knowledge' which have poured into the new liturgies, to say nothing of the 'new forms of culture' that provide its social setting. The outward manifestations do not conceal an inward and spiritual reality; they merely cloak it. As Irenaeus himself taught long ago, 'our bodies, after partaking of the Eucharist, are no longer corruptible, having the hope of eternal resurrection'.[9] As forgiven, nurtured and fed, the eucharistic community is sent out equipped to be more faithful disciples, becoming what we are, the Body of Christ himself. The Eucharist is, therefore, about making us fit for heaven, which means that it is far more than a social construct. It has a life of its own. Every age has therefore to make its own decisions, in the light of the past, about how that celebration should go forward.

Lessons from history tell us that if we wait too long to change things, we risk throwing out too much, whereas if we change too much too often, we provide a milieu of perpetual instability. It could be, for example, that in the future the Eucharist may have more than three readings, as Egeria observed in Jerusalem in the late fourth century; or that the Peace becomes part of a powerful rite of reconciliation and forgiveness; or that the eucharistic prayer bulges with so much creativity that it has to break down into smaller single units. All that may or may not lie ahead, as the Church realizes its mission not only in *laying* the eucharistic table, but in *gathering* people around it.

Underneath this constant journey of the People of God must be a response of faith and trust in the future itself – which is God's future. This means trusting a future generation to put right our mistakes – as well as probably making new ones of their own. It means realizing that we are essentially 'stewards of God's mysteries' (1 Cor. 4.1), worshipping provisionally but faithfully on earth, proclaiming the crucified Lord in a suffering and broken world, until, in the words of Geoffrey Wainwright, 'when the Mystery of God has been completed (Rev. 10.7), sacraments will cease and the Eucharist will give way to the vision of God in His incontestable kingdom'.[10]

NOTES

Chapter 1 Shape

1 Gregory Dix, *The Shape of the Liturgy*, London: Dacre, 1945.
2 See, in general, *Eucharistic Presidency: A Theological Statement by the House of Bishops of the General Synod*, London: Church House Publishing, 1992; see also Peter M. Waddell, 'The eucharistic priesthood of the ordained ministry: a contemporary Anglican proposal', Cambridge University, unpublished PhD dissertation, 2002.
3 Jeremy S. Begbie, *Theology, Music and Time*, Cambridge Studies in Christian Doctrine, Cambridge: Cambridge University Press, 2000, pp. 166ff.
4 Quoted in Gordon W. Lathrop, *Holy Things: A Liturgical Theology*, Minneapolis: Fortress, 1993, p. 10.
5 Dix, *Shape of the Liturgy*, p. 48.
6 See Paul F. Bradshaw, *The Search for the Origins of Christian Worship*, London: SPCK, 1992, esp. pp. 80–130.
7 See, for example, David Brown, *Tradition and Imagination: Revelation and Change*, Oxford: Oxford University Press, 1999, pp. 9–59.
8 Lathrop, *Holy Things*, p. 11.

Chapter 2 Contexts

1 See Michael Perham, *New Handbook of Pastoral Liturgy*, London: SPCK, 2000, esp. pp. 103ff.
2 *Common Worship: Services and Prayers*, p. 166.
3 See Kenneth Stevenson and Bryan Spinks (eds), *The Identity of Anglican Worship*, London: Mowbray, 1991.
4 *First Apology* 67.1; text in R. C. D. Jasper and G. J. Cuming,

Prayers of the Eucharist: Early and Reformed, New York: Pueblo, 1988 (hereafter referred to as *Prayers of the Eucharist*), pp. 29–30.

5 *Ordo Romano Primus* 12; text in *Prayers of the Eucharist*, p. 169.

6 Thomas Frederick Simmons (ed.), *The Lay Folks Mass Book*, Early English Text Society, Oxford: Oxford University Press, 1879, p. 9.

7 Aidan Kavanagh, *Elements of Rite: A Handbook of Liturgical Style*, New York: Pueblo, 1980, p. 31.

8 See Walter J. Ong, *Orality and Literacy: The technologizing of the Word*, London and New York: Methuen, 1982.

Chapter 3 *Variables*

1 Frank C. Senn, *New Creation: A Liturgical Worldview*, Minneapolis: Fortress, 2000, pp. 98ff.

2 Dix, *Shape of the Liturgy*, p. 744.

Chapter 4 *Soft Points*

1 Robert F. Taft, 'How liturgies grow: the evolution of the Byzantine divine liturgy', in *Beyond East and West: Problems in Liturgical Understanding*, New Studies in Church Music and Liturgy, Washington DC: Pastoral Press, 1984, pp. 168ff.; see also Kenneth Stevenson, 'Soft points in the eucharist', in Michael Perham (ed.), *Liturgy for a New Century: Further Essays in Preparation for the Revision of the Alternative Service Book*, Alcuin Club Collection 70, London: SPCK, 1991, pp. 29–43.

2 See Paul F. Bradshaw (ed.), *Companion to Common Worship*, vol 1, Alcuin Club Collection 78, London: SPCK, 2001, p. 130.

3 This is an important point that is consistently overlooked in the debates surrounding what is the appropriate language for prayers at this stage in the Eucharist; see David R. Holeton's essay, 'The sacramental language of S. Leo the Great. A study of the words "munus" and "oblata"', in *Ephemerides Liturgicae* 92 (1978), pp. 115–65.

4 Taft, 'How liturgies grow', p. 168.

5 Bernhard Lang, *Sacred Games: A History of Christian*

Worship, New Haven and London: Yale University Press, 1997, p. 134.

Chapter 5 Symbolism

1 See Frances Young (ed.), *Encounter with Mystery: Reflections on L'Arche and Living with Disability*, London: DLT, 1997.
2 See Dietrich Bonhoeffer, *Ethics*, Fontana Library, London: Collins, 1963.
3 T. Fawcett, *The Symbolic Language of Religion: An Introductory Study*, London: SPCK, 1970, pp. 13–37; see also Duncan Forester, James I. H. McDonald and Gian Tellini (eds), *Encounter with God*, Edinburgh, T&T Clark, 1983, pp. 36–43.
4 David N. Power, *Unsearchable Riches: The Symbolic Nature of Liturgy*, New York: Pueblo, 1984, p. 63.
5 Richard Hooker, *Treatise on the Laws of Ecclesiastical Polity*, V.67.1.
6 See Kenneth Stevenson, *Eucharist and Offering*, New York: Pueblo, 1986, p. 236.
7 *De Sacramentis Christianae Fidei* i.8, vi.466, quoted in Power, *Unsearchable Riches*, pp. 55f.
8 I am indebted to the Revd Robert Sanday, Chaplain to the Deaf in Hampshire and the Isle of Wight, for several insights on disability in this chapter.

Chapter 6 Remembrance

1 *Modern Eucharistic Agreement*, London: SPCK, 1973, pp. 27f. The World Council of Churches Faith and Order Commission worked on similar lines: 'The eucharist is the memorial of the crucified and risen Christ, i.e. the living and effective sign of his sacrifice, accomplished once and for all on the cross and still operative on behalf of all mankind'; see *Baptism, Eucharist and Ministry*, Faith and Order Paper No. 111, Geneva: World Council of Churches, 1982, p. 11.
2 Bertram Doble (ed.), *Centuries of Meditations by Thomas Traherne*, London: Doble, 1908, pp. 70f.
3 Timothy Gorringe, *The Sign of Love: Reflections on the Eucharist*, London: SPCK, 1997, p. 86.

4 From an unpublished discourse; see Westminster Abbey Library, Th Ms 2/1/4, p. 1
5 Hooker, *Laws*, V.67.1.
6 A. M. Ramsey, *The Gospel and the Catholic Church*, London: Longmans, 1936, p. 117.
7 'Pleading' appears in several Anglican writers across the spectrum, including Patrick, Gore, McAdoo, and the Reply of the Bishops to 'Apostolicae Curae', 1897; see *Covenant of Grace Renewed: A Vision of the Eucharist in the Seventeenth Century*, London: DLT, 1994, pp. 16 (n. 40); on the Scottish Reformed tradition, see Bryan D. Spinks, 'The ascension and the vicarious humanity of Christ: The christology and soteriology behind the Church of Scotland's anamnesis and epiklesis', in J. Neil Alexander (ed.), *Time and Community: In Honor of Thomas Julian Talley*, Washington: Pastoral Press, 1990, pp. 185–201.
8 Augustine, *The City of God* X,6.

Chapter 7 Presence

1 George Steiner, *Real Presences*, London: Faber, 1989, pp. 8, 9, 10.
2 Jeremy Taylor, *The Worthy Communicant*, London: Norton, 1660, p. 8.
3 Ramsey, *The Gospel and the Catholic Church*, p. 111.
4 See Chapter 14.
5 Hooker, *Laws*, V.67.11.
6 See *Modern Eucharistic Agreement*, p. 28.
7 F. E. Hutchinson (ed.), *The Works of George Herbert*, Oxford: Clarendon Press, 1945, pp. 200–1.

Chapter 8 Kingdom

1 John and Charles Wesley, *Hymns on the Lord's Supper*, Bristol: Farley, 1784, no. CI (also in *Hymns Ancient and Modern Revised*).
2 Taylor, *Worthy Communicant*, pp. 74f.
3 Richard Godfrey Parsons, *The Sacrament of Sacrifice*, London: Longmans, 1936, p. 62. There are five stanzas in all (five appear in *Hymns Ancient and Modern Revised* and *Hymns*

Ancient and Modern New Standard, whereas only the first four appear in *New English Hymnal*).

4 Emil Nolde, *Last Supper*, London: Phaidon, 2000, pp. 194–5.

5 Mary Astell, *The Christian Religion as Profess'd by a Daughter of the Church of England*, London, 1705, p. 158, quoted in Geoffrey Rowell, Kenneth Stevenson and Rowan Williams (eds), *Love's Redeeming Work: The Anglican Quest for Holiness*, Oxford: Oxford University Press, 2001, p. 261.

6 See Christopher Cocksworth, *Evangelical Eucharistic Thought in the Church of England*, Cambridge: Cambridge University Press, 1993.

Chapter 9 Approach

1 Timothy Fawcett, *The Liturgy of Comprehension 1689*, Alcuin Club Collections 54, Southend-on-Sea: Mayhew-McCrimmon, 1973, pp. 102–3.

2 Bishop E. R. Morgan (ed.), *Reginald Somerset Ward: His Life and Letters*, London: Mowbrays, 1963, p. 83.

3 Simon Patrick, *Mensa Mystica: Or, a Discourse Concerning the Sacrament of the Lord's Supper*, London: Tyton, 1684, p. 158; the first edition appeared in 1660.

4 Justin Martyr, *First Apology* 67.1, *Prayers of the Eucharist*, p. 28.

5 Robert W. Hovda, *Strong, Loving and Wise: Presiding in the Liturgy*, Collegeville: Liturgical Press, 1976, p. 8.

6 Kavanagh, *Elements of Rite*, p. 77.

7 *The Sermons of Lancelot Andrewes*, Library of Anglo-Catholic Theology, Oxford: Parker, 1843, p. 101; see Kenneth W. Stevenson, '"Human Nature Honoured": absolution in Lancelot Andrewes', in Martin R Dudley (ed.), *Like a Two-Edged Sword: The Word of God in Liturgy and History – Essays in Honour of Canon Donald Gray*, Norwich: Canterbury Press, 1995, pp. 113–37.

Chapter 10 Word

1 Timothy Fry (ed.), *The Rule of St Benedict in Latin and English with Notes*, Collegeville: Liturgical Press, 1981, pp. 156–7.

2 Mark Santer, *The Church's Sacrifice*, Fairacres Publication 47, Oxford: SLG Press, 1975, p. 3.

3 Henry Walter (ed.), *Doctrinal Treatises by William Tyndale*, Parker Society, Cambridge: Cambridge University Press, 1948, p. 9.

4 See above Chapter 2, pp. 16–17.

5 See John Wilkinson, *Egeria's Travels*, London: SPCK, 1971; second and third editions published by Aris and Phillips, 1981 and 1999.

6 See Kenneth Stevenson, 'Animal rites: the four living creatures in patristic exegesis and liturgy', *Studia Patristica* XXXIV, pp. 470–92.

7 O. C. Edwards, Jr, *Elements of Homiletic: A Method for Preparing to Preach*, New York: Pueblo, 1982, p. 17.

Chapter 11 Creed

1 See E. C. Whitaker, *Documents of the Baptismal Liturgy*, London: SPCK, 1970, pp. 5–6 and G. J. Cuming, *Hippolytus: A Text for Students*, Grove Liturgical Study 8, Bramcote: Grove, 1976, pp. 19–20.

2 F. D. Maurice, *The Kingdom of Christ; or Hints to a Quaker*, Vol. II, London: Rivingtons, 1842, p. 24.

3 Wolfhart Pannenberg, *The Apostles' Creed in the Light of Today's Questions*, London: SCM Press, 1972. pp. 4–5.

Chapter 12 Intercession

1 Book 1.1 (1), in Henry Chadwick (tr.), *Saint Augustine: Confessions*, Oxford: Clarendon Press, 1991, p. 3.

2 See Kenneth Stevenson, *Abba, Father: Using and Interpreting the Lord's Prayer*, Norwich: Canterbury Press, 2000.

3 See, for example, *Common Worship: Prayers and Services*, p. 214.

4 Jack Nicholls, 'The Prayers of the People', in Stephen Conway (ed.), *Living the Eucharist: Affirming Catholicism and the Liturgy*, London: DLT, 2001, pp. 72f.

5 Peter Baelz, *Prayer and Providence*, London: SCM Press, 1968, p. 101.

6 Somerset Ward, *To Jerusalem*, p. 129.
7 See Kenneth Stevenson, "'Ye shall pray for . . .": The Intercession', in *Liturgy Reshaped*, London: SPCK, 1982, pp. 46–7
   (whole essay, pp. 32–47).
8 Letter to *The Times*, 25 May 1995.
9 Dietrich Bonhoeffer, *Sanctorum Communio*, London: Collins,
   1963, pp. 132–3; *Sanctorum Communio* was originally written as a doctoral dissertation at Berlin in 1927, and was first
   published in German in 1930.

Chapter 13 Peace and Offering

1 Justin Martyr, *First Apology* 65.1; text in *Prayers of the
   Eucharist*, p. 28.
2 See, for example, *Common Worship: Services and Prayers*,
   p. 175.
3 See Chapter 4, pp. 36–40.
4 *The Book of Common Order* (1940). Edinburgh, Glasgow,
   London: Oxford University Press, 1940, p. 118.
5 Colin Buchanan, *The Kiss of Peace*, Grove Worship Series 80,
   Bramcote: Grove, 1982, p. 3.
6 Cyril of Jerusalem, *Mystagogical Catecheses* 5.3, in F. L. Cross
   (tr.), *St Cyril of Jerusalem's Lectures on the Christian
   Sacraments*, London: SPCK, 1951, p. 72; see Buchanan, *The
   Kiss of Peace*, p. 9.
7 Augustine, *Sermons* 227, translated by Buchanan, *The Kiss of
   Peace*, p. 11.
8 Alan Bennett, 'Comfortable Words', in *Writing Home*,
   London: Faber, 1994, p. 356.
9 *Hymns Ancient and Modern Revised* 210.
10 *Didache* 9, text in *Prayers of the Eucharist*, p. 23.

Chapter 14 The Eucharistic Prayer

1 *Didache* 9, text in *Prayers of the Eucharist*, p. 23.
2 See discussion and texts in *Prayers of the Eucharist*, pp. 7–10.
3 See *Baptism, Eucharist and Ministry*, pp. 10–13; the influence
   of Max Thurian is clear: *L'Eucharistie: Mémorial du Seigneur,
   Sacrifice d'action de grâce et d'intercession*, Neuchâtel, Paris:

Delachaux et Niestlé, 1959, and 'The Eucharistic Memorial, Sacrifice of Praise and Supplication', in Max Thurian (ed.), *Ecumenical Perspectives on Baptism Eucharist and Ministry*, Faith and Order Paper 116, Geneva: World Council Churches, 1983, pp. 90–103.

4 See, for example, Bradshaw, *The Search for the Origins*, pp. 1–29, for an excellent investigation into this whole debate, in which a number of important cautions are registered about Jewish liturgy as an evolving tradition even in the time of Christ.

5 See the Excursus on Eucharistic Prayers, following this chapter.

6 See the chart in Bradshaw (ed.), *Companion to Common Worship* Vol. 1, p. 139.

7 *Hom. 17 in Heb. 3*, in Henry Bettenson (ed. and tr.), *The Later Christian Fathers*, London: Oxford University Press, 1970, p. 174.

8 *Prayers of the Eucharist*, p. 133.

9 See *Ninety-Six Sermons by Lancelot Andrewes* Vol. 2, Library of Anglo-Catholic Theology, Oxford: Parker, 1841, p. 299.

10 Irenaeus, *Adversus Haereses*, IV.xviii.5, in Henry Bettenson (ed. and tr.), *The Early Christian Fathers: A Selection from the Writings of the Fathers from St Clement of Rome to St Athanasius*, Oxford: Oxford University Press, 1969, p. 96.

11 See Bryan D. Spinks, *The Sanctus in the Eucharistic Prayer*, Cambridge: Cambridge University Press, 1991, for the most extensive study.

Excursus: *The Eight Eucharistic Prayers*

1 Basil of Caesarea, *De Spiritu Sancto* 27.66, in *St Basil the Great On the Holy Spirit*, New York: St Vladimir's Seminary, 1970, p. 99.

2 Karl Rahner, *The Church and the Sacraments*, London: Burns and Oates, 1974, p. 85.

3 See Bradshaw, *Companion to Common Worship* Vol. 1, pp. 137–44; Perham, *New Handbook*, pp. 131–4; and Colin Buchanan and Charles Read, *The Eucharistic Prayers of Order One*, Grove Worship Booklet 158, Bramcote: Grove, 2000.

4 See *Prayers of the Eucharist*, p. 35.

5 *Patterns for Worship: A Report by the Liturgical Commission*

of the General Synod of the Church of England, London: Church House Publishing, 1989, pp. 239–51.

6 Buchanan and Read, *Eucharistic Prayers*, p. 17.

7 Buchanan and Read, *Eucharistic Prayers*, p. 19.

8 See also *Eucharistic Prayer of Saint Basil: Text for Consultation*, Washington: International Commission on English in the Liturgy, 1985, which tried to go further than the 'ecumenical' version that appeared in BCP (1979) and BAS (1985), and included also responses throughout.

9 *An Original Eucharistic Prayer: Text 1*, Washington: International Commission on English in the Liturgy, 1984.

10 *Patterns for Worship*, pp. 243–7.

11 See H. R. McAdoo and Kenneth Stevenson, *The Mystery of the Eucharist in the Anglican Tradition*, Norwich: Canterbury Press, 1995, 1997, pp. 144ff.; see also Chapter 6, n. 7.

12 'The tranquil night, /At the time of the rising of the dawn, /The silent music, the sounding solitude, /The supper that recreates and enkindles love.' See E. Allison Peers (tr. and ed.), *The Complete Works of Saint John of the Cross*, London: Burns and Oates, 1964, p. 72.

13 Kenneth Kirk, *The Vision of God: The Christian Doctrine of the Summum Bonum*, London: Longmans, 1931; on 2 October 1991, the petition for the departed at conventual mass at Quarr Abbey, Isle of Wight, consisted of the words, 'may they enjoy the vision of God for which they were created'.

14 Augustine, *Confessions* I.i (1); see also Chapter 12, n. 1, where it is quoted; and Hutchinson, *Works of George Herbert*, pp. 188–9.

15 There is clearly scope for further such prefaces, e.g. for Religious, Dedication, Baptism and Confirmation; some existing texts could be adapted from Alan Griffiths, *We Give You Thanks and Praise: The Ambrosian Eucharistic Prefaces*, Norwich: Canterbury Press, 1999.

Chapter 15 Communion

1 See Stevenson, *Abba, Father*; see also Chapter 4 on its use as a background to intercession.

2 See Colin Buchanan, *The Lord's Prayer in the Church of England*, Grove Worship Booklet 13, Bramcote: Grove, 1995;

this excellent little study should have been included in the bibliography to my *Abba, Father,* and I gladly salute it here.

3 *Didache* 8.2; see also Stevenson, *Abba, Father,* pp. 113ff.

4 See Kenneth Stevenson, *Covenant of Grace Renewed: A Vision of the Eucharist in the Seventeenth Century,* London: DLT, 1994, pp. 50f.

5 Text in *Prayers of the Eucharist,* pp. 274–5.

6 It is referred to as 'this Collect of humble access to the holy Communion' in the 1637 Scottish Liturgy; see Gordon Donaldson, *The Making of the Scottish Prayer Book of 1637,* Edinburgh: Edinburgh University Press, 1954, p. 200.

7 See *The Prayers and Meditations of St Anselm with the Proslogion,* translated with an introduction by Sister Benedicta Ward, SLG, London: Penguin Books, 1973, p. 100; see also Kenneth Stevenson, ' "Somewhere behind the world of sensible appearances": the liturgy as contextual, devotional, trinitarian, and baptismal', in Joanne Pierce and Michael Downey (eds), *Source and Summit: Commemorating Josef A. Jungmann, SJ,* Collegeville: Liturgical Press, 1999, pp. 124f. (whole essay, pp. 121–31).

8 See *Baudouin de Ford: Le Sacrement de L'Autel I,* Sources Chrétiennes 93, Paris: Éditions du Cerf, 1963, pp.128–9 (*De Sacramento Altaris* 11.2).

Chapter 16 Conclusion

1 See Thomas Schattauer, 'The Koinonicon of the Byzantine Liturgy: an historical study', in *Orientalia Christiana Periodica* 49.1 (1983), pp. 109–10 (whole article, pp. 91–120).

2 See David F. Ford, *Self and Salvation: Being Transformed,* Cambridge Studies in Christian Doctrine, Cambridge: Cambridge University Press, 1999, pp. 137ff.

3 Ford, *Self and Salvation,* pp. 162–6.

4 Dietrich Bonhoeffer, *Life Together,* London: SCM Press, 1954, p. 96.

5 See Allison Peters (tr.), *Way of Perfection: Saint Teresa of Avila,* London: Sheed and Ward, 1999, p. 148 (Chaper 34).

6 See *The Christian Year: Collects and Post Communion Prayers for Sundays and Festivals,* London: Church House Publishing, 1997, pp. 249–59.

7 *The Works of Christina Rossetti*, Wordsworth Poetry Library, Ware: Wordsworth Editions, 1995, p. 266.

Epilogue: What of the Future?

1 David N. Power, *The Eucharistic Mystery: Revitalizing the Tradition*, New York: Crossroad, 1992, p. 326.

2 See, for example, David Ford's discussion of 'selfhood' in Paul Ricoeur, *Self and Salvation*, pp. 82ff.

3 Rowan Williams, *Lost Icons: Reflections on Cultural Bereavement*, Edinburgh: T&T Clark, 2000, pp. 109ff.

4 See B. A. Gerrish, *Grace and Gratitude: The Eucharistic Theology of John Calvin*, Edinburgh: T&T Clark, 1993.

5 See the important work of David Kennedy, 'The epiclesis in the eucharistic rites of the Church of England and the churches of the Anglican Communion with special reference to the period 1900–1994', Birmingham University, unpublished PhD thesis, 1996.

6 See Robert Sokolowski, *Eucharistic Presence: A Study in the Theology of Disclosure*, Washington: Catholic University of America Press, 1994, p. 28.

7 Lucy Menzies (ed.), *The Collected Papers of Evelyn Underhill*, London: Longmans, 1946, p. 198.

8 David Brown, *Discipleship and Imagination: Christian Tradition and Truth*, Oxford: Oxford University Press, 2000, p. 405.

9 See Chapter 14, n. 10; *Adversus Haereses* IV.xviii.5

10 Geoffrey Wainwright, *Eucharist and Eschatology*, London: Epworth, 1971, p. 154.

INDEX OF NAMES

INDEX OF SUBJECTS